A Practitioner's Guide to Software Test Design

Lee Copeland

Artech House
Publishers

Boston • London

A Practitioner's Guide to Software Test Design

Library of Congress and British CIP information available on request

Artech House Publishers

685 Canton Street	46 Gillingham Street
Norwood, MA 02062	London SW1V 1AH
(781) 769-9750	+44 (0)20 7596-8750
www.artechhouse.com	

International Standard Book Number:
1-58053-791-X
978-1-58053-791-9

Printed in the United States of America

Seventh Printing: February 2007

Trademarks

All terms mentioned in this book that are known to be trademarks or service marks have been appropriately capitalized. Artech House Publishers and STQE Publishing cannot attest to the accuracy of this information. Use of a term in this book should not be regarded as affecting the validity of any trademark or service mark.

Warning and Disclaimer

Every effort has been made to make this book as complete and accurate as possible, but no warranty or fitness is implied. The information provided is on an "as is" basis. The authors and the publisher shall have neither liability nor responsibility to any person or entity with respect to any loss or damages arising from the information contained in this book.

Dedication

To my wife Suzanne, and our wonderful children and grandchildren

Shawn and Martha
    Andrew and Cassandra
David
Cathleen
    Katelynn and Kiley
Melissa and Jay
    Ross, Elizabeth, and Miranda
Brian and Heather
    Cassidy and Caden
Thomas and Jeni
Carrie
Sundari
Rajan

and to Wayne, Jerry, Dani, Ron, and Rayanne for their encouragement over the years.

Table of Contents

Preface

A Practitioner's Guide to Software Test Design contains today's important current test design approaches in one unique book. Until now, software testers had to search through a number of books, periodicals, and Web sites to locate this vital information.

The book focuses only on software test design, not related subjects such as test planning, test management, test team development, etc. While those are important in software testing, they have often overshadowed what testers really need—the more practical aspects of testing, specifically test case design. Other excellent books can guide you through the overall process of software testing. One of my favorites is *Systematic Software Testing* by Rick Craig and Stefan Jaskiel.

A Practitioner's Guide to Software Test Design illustrates each test design approach through detailed examples and step-by-step instructions. These lead the reader to a clear understanding of each test design technique.

■■■■■■■■■■■■■■■■■■
Importance of Test Design

"The act of careful, complete, systematic, test design will catch as many bugs as the act of testing. ... Personally, I believe that it's far more effective."
- Boris Beizer

Today's Testing Challenges

For any system of interesting size it is impossible to test all the different logic paths and all the different input data combinations. Of the infinite number of choices, each one of which is worthy of some level of testing, testers can only choose a very small subset because of resource constraints. The purpose of this book is to help you analyze, design, and choose such subsets, to implement those tests that are most likely to discover defects.

It is vital to choose test cases wisely. Missing a defect can result in significant losses to your organization if a defective system is placed into production.

A Practitioner's Guide to Software Test Design describes a set of key test design strategies that improve both the efficiency and effectiveness of software testers.

Structure and Approach

A Practitioner's Guide to Software Test Design explains the most important test design techniques in use today. Some of these techniques are classics and well known throughout the testing community. Some have been around for a while but are not well known among test engineers. Still others are not widely known, but should be because of their effectiveness. This book brings together all these techniques into one volume, helping the test designer become more efficient and effective in testing.

Each test design technique is approached from a practical, rather than a theoretical basis. Each test design technique is first introduced through a simple example, then explained in detail. When possible, additional examples of its use are presented. The types of problems on which the approach can be used, along with its limitations, are described. Each test design technique chapter ends with a summary of its key points, along with exercises the reader can use for practice, and references for further reading. Testers can use the techniques presented immediately on their projects.

■■■■■■■■■■■■■■■■■■
A Note from the Author

I love a good double integral sign

$$\iint$$

as much as the next tester, but we're going to concentrate on the practical, not the theoretical.

Each test design approach is described in a self-contained chapter. Because the chapters are focused, concise, and independent they can be read "out of order." Testers can read the chapters that are most relevant to their work at the moment.

Audience

This book was written specifically for:

- Software test engineers who have the primary responsibility for test case design. This book details the most efficient and effective methods for creating test cases.

- Software developers who, with the advent of Extreme Programming and other agile development methods, are being asked to do more and better testing of the software they write. Many developers have not been exposed to the design techniques described in this book.

- Test and development managers who must understand, at least in principle, the work their staff performs. Not only does this book provide an overview of important test design methods, it will assist managers in estimating the effort, time, and cost of good testing.

- Quality assurance and process improvement engineers who are charged with defining and improving their software testing process.

- Instructors and professors who are searching for an excellent reference for a course in software test design techniques.

Appreciation

The following reviewers have provided invaluable assistance in the writing of this book: Anne Meilof, Chuck Allison, Dale Perry, Danny Faught, Dorothy Graham, Geoff Quentin, James Bach, Jon Hagar, Paul Gerrard, Rex Black, Rick Craig, Robert Rose-Coutré, Sid Snook, and Wayne Middleton. My sincere thanks to each of them. Any faults in this book should be attributed directly to them. (Just kidding!)

Some Final Comments

This book contains a number of references to Web sites. These references were correct when the manuscript was submitted to the publisher. Unfortunately, they may have become broken by the time the book is in the readers' hands.

It has become standard practice for authors to include a pithy quotation on the title page of each chapter. Unfortunately, the practice has become so prevalent that all the good quotations have been used. Just for fun, I have chosen instead to include on each chapter title page a winning entry from the 2003 Bulwer-Lytton Fiction Contest (http://www.bulwer-lytton.com). Since 1982, the English Department at San Jose State University has sponsored this event, a competition that challenges writers to compose the opening sentence to the <u>worst</u> of all possible novels. It was inspired by Edward George Bulwer-Lytton who began his novel *Paul Clifford* with:

> "It was a dark and stormy night; the rain fell in torrents—except at occasional intervals, when it was checked by a violent gust of wind which

swept up the streets (for it is in London that our
scene lies), rattling along the housetops, and
fiercely agitating the scanty flame of the lamps
that struggled against the darkness."

My appreciation to Dr. Scott Rice of San Jose State University
for permission to use these exemplary illustrations of bad
writing. Hopefully, nothing in this book will win this prestigious
award.

Acknowledgements

The caricature of Mick Jagger is owned and copyrighted by
Martin O'Loughlin and used by permission.
Clip Art copyright by Corel Corporation and used under a
licensing agreement.

References

Beizer, Boris (1990). *Software Testing Techniques* (Second
Edition). Van Nostrand Reinhold.

Craig, Rick D. and Stefan P. Jaskiel (2002). *Systematic Software
Testing*. Artech House Publishers.

Chapter 1 –
The Testing Process

The flock of geese flew overhead in a 'V' formation—not in an old-fashioned-looking Times New Roman kind of a 'V', branched out slightly at the two opposite arms at the top of the 'V', nor in a more modern-looking, straight and crisp, linear Arial sort of 'V' (although since they were flying, Arial might have been appropriate), but in a slightly asymmetric, tilting off-to-one-side sort of italicized Courier New-like 'V'—and LaFonte knew that he was just the type of man to know the difference.[*]

— John Dotson

---

[*] If you think this quotation has nothing to do with software testing you are correct. For an explanation please read "Some Final Comments" in the Preface.

Testing

What is testing? While many definitions have been written, at its core testing is the process of comparing "what is" with "what ought to be." A more formal definition is given in the IEEE Standard 610.12-1990, "IEEE Standard Glossary of Software Engineering Terminology" which defines "testing" as:

> "The process of operating a system or component under specified conditions, observing or recording the results, and making an evaluation of some aspect of the system or component."

The "specified conditions" referred to in this definition are embodied in test cases, the subject of this book.

Rick Craig and Stefan Jaskiel propose an expanded definition of software testing in their book, *Systematic Software Testing*.

> "Testing is a concurrent lifecycle process of engineering, using and maintaining testware in order to measure and improve the quality of the software being tested."

This view includes the planning, analysis, and design that leads to the creation of test cases in addition to the IEEE's focus on test execution.

Different organizations and different individuals have varied views of the purpose of software testing. Boris Beizer describes five levels of testing maturity. (He called them phases but today we know the politically correct term is "levels" and there are always five of them.)

■■■■■■■■■■■■■■■■■
Key Point

At its core, testing is the process of comparing "what is" with "what ought to be."

Level 0 – "There's no difference between testing and debugging. Other than in support of debugging, testing has no purpose." Defects may be stumbled upon but there is no formalized effort to find them.

Level 1 – "The purpose of testing is to show that software works." This approach, which starts with the premise that the software is (basically) correct, may blind us to discovering defects. Glenford Myers wrote that those performing the testing may subconsciously select test cases that should not fail. They will not create the "diabolical" tests needed to find deeply hidden defects.

Level 2 – "The purpose of testing is to show that the software doesn't work." This is a very different mindset. It assumes the software doesn't work and challenges the tester to find its defects. With this approach, we will consciously select test cases that evaluate the system in its nooks and crannies, at its boundaries, and near its edges, using diabolically constructed test cases.

Level 3 – "The purpose of testing is not to prove anything, but to reduce the perceived risk of not working to an acceptable value." While we can prove a system incorrect with only one test case, it is impossible to ever prove it correct. To do so would require us to test every possible valid combination of input data and every possible invalid combination of input data. Our goals are to understand the quality of the software in terms of its defects, to furnish the programmers with information about the software's deficiencies, and to provide management with an evaluation of the negative impact on our organization if we shipped this system to customers in its present state.

Level 4 – "Testing is not an act. It is a mental discipline that results in low-risk software without much testing effort." At this maturity level we focus on making software more testable from its inception. This includes reviews and inspections of its requirements, design, and code. In addition, it means writing code that incorporates facilities the tester can easily use to interrogate it while it is executing. Further, it means writing code that is self-diagnosing, that reports errors rather than requiring testers to discover them.

Current Challenges

When I ask my students about the challenges they face in testing they typically reply:

- Not enough time to test properly
- Too many combinations of inputs to test
- Not enough time to test well
- Difficulty in determining the expected results of each test
- Nonexistent or rapidly changing requirements
- Not enough time to test thoroughly
- No training in testing processes
- No tool support
- Management that either doesn't understand testing or (apparently) doesn't care about quality
- Not enough time

This book does not contain "magic pixie dust" that you can use to create additional time, better requirements, or more enlightened management. It does, however, contain techniques that will make you more efficient and effective in your testing by helping you choose and construct test cases that will find substantially more defects than you have in the past while using fewer resources.

Test Cases

To be most effective and efficient, test cases must be designed, not just slapped together. The word "design" has a number of definitions:

1. To conceive or fashion in the mind; invent: *design a good reason to attend the STAR testing conference.* To formulate a plan for; devise: *design a marketing strategy for the new product.*
2. To plan out in systematic, usually documented form: *design a building; design a test case.*
3. To create or contrive for a particular purpose or effect: *a game designed to appeal to all ages.*
4. To have as a goal or purpose; intend.
5. To create or execute in an artistic or highly skilled manner.

Each of these definitions applies to good test case design. Regarding test case design, Roger Pressman wrote:

"The design of tests for software and other engineering products can be as challenging as the initial design of the product itself. Yet ... software engineers often treat testing as an afterthought, developing test cases that 'feel right' but have little assurance of being complete. Recalling the objectives of testing, we must design tests that have the highest likelihood of finding the most errors with a minimum amount of time and effort."

Well designed test cases are composed of three parts:

■■■■■■■■■■■■■■■■■
Key Point

Test cases consist
of inputs, outputs,
and order of
execution.

- Inputs
- Outputs
- Order of execution

Inputs

Inputs are commonly thought of as data entered at a keyboard. While that is a significant source of system input, data can come from other sources—data from interfacing systems, data from interfacing devices, data read from files or databases, the state the system is in when the data arrives, and the environment within which the system executes.

Outputs

Outputs have this same variety. Often outputs are thought of as just the data displayed on a computer screen. In addition, data can be sent to interfacing systems and to external devices. Data can be written to files or databases. The state or the environment may be modified by the system's execution.

All of these relevant inputs and outputs are important components of a test case. In test case design, determining the expected outputs is the function of an "oracle."

An oracle is any program, process, or data that provides the test designer with the expected result of a test. Beizer lists five types of oracles:

- Kiddie Oracles – Just run the program and see what comes out. If it looks about right, it must be right.

- Regression Test Suites – Run the program and compare the output to the results of the same tests run against a previous version of the program.

- Validated Data – Run the program and compare the results against a standard such as a table, formula, or other accepted definition of valid output.

- Purchased Test Suites – Run the program against a standardized test suite that has been previously created and validated. Programs like compilers, Web browsers, and SQL (Structured Query Language) processors are often tested against such suites.

- Existing Program – Run the program and compare the output to another version of the program.

Order of Execution

There are two styles of test case design regarding order of test execution.

- Cascading test cases – Test cases may build on each other. For example, the first test case exercises a particular feature of the software and then leaves the system in a state such that the second test case can be executed. In testing a database consider these test cases:

    1. Create a record
    2. Read the record
    3. Update the record
    4. Read the record
    5. Delete the record
    6. Read the deleted record

Each of these tests could be built on the previous tests. The advantage is that each test case is typically smaller and simpler. The disadvantage is that if one test fails, the subsequent tests may be invalid.

- Independent test cases – Each test case is entirely self contained. Tests do not build on each other or require that other tests have been successfully executed. The advantage is that any number of tests can be executed in any order. The disadvantage is that each test tends to be larger and more complex and thus more difficult to design, create, and maintain.

Types Of Testing

Testing is often divided into black box testing and white box testing.

Black box testing is a strategy in which testing is based solely on the requirements and specifications. Unlike its complement, white box testing, black box testing requires no knowledge of the internal paths, structure, or implementation of the software under test.

White box testing is a strategy in which testing is based on the internal paths, structure, and implementation of the software under test. Unlike its complement, black box testing, white box testing generally requires detailed programming skills.

An additional type of testing is called gray box testing. In this approach we peek into the "box" under test just long enough to understand how it has been implemented. Then we close up the box and use our knowledge to choose more effective black box tests.

Testing Levels

Typically testing, and therefore test case design, is performed at four different levels:

Key Point

The classical testing levels are unit, integration, system, and acceptance.

- Unit Testing – A unit is the "smallest" piece of software that a developer creates. It is typically the work of one programmer and is stored in a single disk file. Different programming languages have different units: In C++ and Java the unit is the class; in C the unit is the function; in less structured languages like Basic and COBOL the unit may be the entire program.

- Integration Testing – In integration we assemble units together into subsystems and finally into systems. It is possible for units to function perfectly in isolation but to fail when integrated. A classic example is this C program and its subsidiary function:

```
/* main program */
void oops(int);
int main() {
oops(42);  /* call the oops function passing an integer */
return 0;
}

/* function oops (in a separate file) */
#include <stdio.h>
void oops(double x) { /* expects a double, not an int! */
printf ("%f\n",x);  /* Will print garbage (0 is most likely) */
}
```

If these units were tested individually, each would appear to function correctly. In this case, the defect only appears when the two units are integrated. The main program passes an integer to function oops but oops expects a double length integer and trouble ensues. It is vital to perform integration testing as the integration process proceeds.

- System Testing – A system consists of all of the software (and possibly hardware, user manuals, training materials, etc.) that make up the product delivered to the customer. System testing focuses on defects that arise at this highest level of integration. Typically system testing includes many types of testing: functionality, usability, security, internationalization and localization, reliability and availability, capacity, performance, backup and recovery, portability, and many more. This book deals only with functionality testing. While the other types of testing are important, they are beyond the scope of this volume.

- Acceptance Testing – Acceptance testing is defined as that testing, which when completed successfully, will result in the customer accepting the software and giving us their money. From the customer's point of view, they would generally like the most exhaustive acceptance testing possible (equivalent to the level of system testing). From the vendor's point of view, we would generally like the minimum level of testing possible that would result in money changing hands. Typical strategic questions that should be addressed before acceptance testing are: Who defines the level of the acceptance testing? Who creates the test scripts? Who executes the tests? What is the pass/fail criteria for the acceptance test? When and how do we get paid?

Not all systems are amenable to using these levels. These levels assume that there is a significant period of time between developing units and integrating them into subsystems and then into systems. In Web development it is often possible to go from concept to code to production in a matter of hours. In that case, the unit-integration-system levels don't make much sense. Many Web testers use an alternate set of levels:

- Code quality
- Functionality
- Usability
- Performance
- Security

The Impossibility Of Testing Everything

In his monumental book *Testing Object-Oriented Systems*, Robert Binder provides an excellent example of the impossibility of testing "everything." Consider the following program:

```
int blech (int j) {
    j = j - 1;          // should be j = j + 1
    j = j / 30000;
    return j;
}
```

Note that the second line is incorrect! The function blech accepts an integer j, subtracts one from it, divides it by 30000 (integer division, whole numbers, no remainder) and returns the value just computed. If integers are implemented using 16 bits on this computer executing this software, the lowest possible input value is −32768 and the highest is 32767. Thus there are 65,536 possible inputs into this tiny program. (Your organization's programs are probably larger.) Will you have the time (and the stamina) to create 65,536 test cases? Of course not. So which input values do we choose? Consider the following input values and their ability to detect this defect.

Input (j)	Expected Result	Actual Result
1	0	0
42	0	0
40000	1	1
-64000	-2	-2

Oops! Note that none of the test cases chosen have detected this defect. In fact only four of the possible 65,536 input values will find this defect. What is the chance that you will choose all four? What is the chance you will choose one of the four? What is the chance you will win the Powerball lottery? Is your answer the same to each of these three questions?

Summary

- Testing is a concurrent lifecycle process of engineering, using, and maintaining testware in order to measure and improve the quality of the software being tested. (Craig and Jaskiel)

- The design of tests for software and other engineering products can be as challenging as the initial design of the product itself. Yet … software engineers often treat testing as an afterthought, developing test cases that 'feel right' but have little assurance of being complete. Recalling the objectives of testing, we must design tests that have the highest likelihood of finding the most errors with a minimum amount of time and effort. (Pressman)

- Black box testing is a strategy in which testing is based solely on the requirements and specifications. White box testing is a strategy in which testing is based on the internal paths, structure, and implementation of the software under test.

- Typically testing, and therefore test case design, is performed at four different levels: Unit, Integration, System, and Acceptance.

Practice

1. Which four inputs to the blech routine will find the hidden defect? How did you determine them? What does this suggest to you as an approach to finding other defects?

References

Beizer, Boris (1990). *Software Testing Techniques* (Second Edition). Van Nostrand Reinhold.

Binder, Robert V. (2000). *Testing Object-Oriented Systems: Models, Patterns, and Tools.* Addison-Wesley.

Craig, Rick D. and Stefan P. Jaskiel (2002). *Systematic Software Testing.* Artech House Publishers.

IEEE Standard 610.12-1990, IEEE Standard Glossary of Software Engineering Terminology, 1991.

Myers, Glenford (1979). *The Art of Software Testing.* John Wiley & Sons.

Pressman, Roger S. (1982). *Software Engineering: A Practitioner's Approach* (Fourth Edition). McGraw-Hill.

Chapter 2 –
Case Studies

They had but one last remaining night together, so they embraced each other as tightly as that two-flavor entwined string cheese that is orange and yellowish-white, the orange probably being a bland Cheddar and the white . . . Mozzarella, although it could possibly be Provolone or just plain American, as it really doesn't taste distinctly dissimilar from the orange, yet they would have you believe it does by coloring it differently.

— Mariann Simms

Why Case Studies?

Two case studies are provided in the appendices of this book. Appendix A describes "Brown & Donaldson," an online brokerage firm. Appendix B describes the "Stateless University Registration System." Examples from these case studies are used to illustrate the test case design techniques described in this book. In addition, some of the book's exercises are based on the case studies. The following sections briefly describe the case studies. Read the detailed information in Appendix A and B when required.

Brown & Donaldson

Brown & Donaldson (B&D) is a **fictitious** online brokerage firm that you can use to practice the test design techniques presented in this book. B&D was originally created for Software Quality Engineering's Web/eBusiness Testing course (for more details see http://www.sqe.com).

Screen shots of various pages are included in Appendix A. Reference will be made to some of these throughout the book. The actual B&D Web site is found at http://bdonline.sqe.com. Any resemblance to any actual online brokerage Web site is purely coincidental.

You can actually try the B&D Web site. First-time users will need to create a BDonline account. **This account is not real—** any transactions requested or executed via this account will **not** occur in the real world, only in the fictitious world of B&D. Once you have created an account, you will bypass this step and login with your username and password. While creating a new account you will be asked to supply an authorization code. The authorization code is eight 1s.

This Web site also contains a number of downloadable documents from the B&D case study, which can be used to assist you in developing test plans for your own Web projects.

Stateless University Registration System

Every state has a state university. This case study describes an online student registration system for the **fictitious** Stateless University. Please do not attempt to cash out your stocks from Brown & Donaldson to enroll at Stateless U.

The document in Appendix B describes the planned user interface for the Stateless University Registration System (SURS). It defines the user interface screens in the order in which they are typically used. It starts with the login screen. Then it provides the data base set-up fields, the addition/change/ deletion of students, the addition/change/deletion of courses, and the addition/change/deletion of class sections. The final data entry screen provides the selection of specific course sections for each student. Additional administrative functions are also defined.

Section I –
Black Box Testing Techniques

Definition

B lack box testing is a strategy in which testing is based solely on the requirements and specifications. Unlike its complement, white box testing, black box testing requires no knowledge of the internal paths, structure, or implementation of the software under test (SUT).

The general black box testing process is:

- The requirements or specifications are analyzed.
- Valid inputs are chosen based on the specification to determine that the SUT processes them correctly. Invalid inputs must also be chosen to verify that the SUT detects them and handles them properly.
- Expected outputs for those inputs are determined.
- Tests are constructed with the selected inputs.
- The tests are run.
- Actual outputs are compared with the expected outputs.
- A determination is made as to the proper functioning of the SUT.

Applicability

Black box testing can be applied at all levels of system development—unit, integration, system, and acceptance.

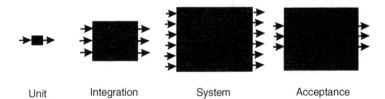

Unit   Integration   System   Acceptance

As we move up in size from module to subsystem to system the box gets larger, with more complex inputs and more complex outputs, but the approach remains the same. Also, as we move up in size, we are forced to the black box approach; there are simply too many paths through the SUT to perform white box testing.

Disadvantages

When using black box testing, the tester can never be sure of how much of the SUT has been tested. No matter how clever or diligent the tester, some execution paths may never be exercised. For example, what is the probability a tester would select a test case to discover this "feature"?

```
if (name=="Lee" && employeeNumber=="1234" &&
employmentStatus=="RecentlyTerminatedForCause") {
send Lee a check for $1,000,000;
}
```

To find every defect using black box testing, the tester would have to create every possible combination of input data, both valid and invalid. This exhaustive input testing is almost always impossible. We can only choose a subset (often a very small subset) of the input combinations.

In *The Art of Software Testing*, Glenford Myers provides an excellent example of the futility of exhaustive testing: How would you thoroughly test a compiler? By writing every possible valid and invalid program. The problem is substantially worse for systems that must remember what has happened before (i.e., that remember their state). In those systems, not only must we test every possible input, we must test every possible sequence of every possible input.

■■■■■■■■■■■■■■■■
Key Point

When using black box testing, the tester can never be sure of how much of the system under test has been tested.

■■■■■■■■■■■■■■■■
Key Point

Even though we can't test everything, formal black box testing directs the tester to choose subsets of tests that are both efficient and effective in finding defects.

Advantages

Even though we can't test everything, formal black box testing directs the tester to choose subsets of tests that are both efficient and effective in finding defects. As such, these subsets will find more defects than a randomly created equivalent number of tests. Black box testing helps maximize the return on our testing investment.

References

Myers, Glenford J. (1979). *The Art of Software Testing*. John Wiley & Sons.

Chapter 3 –
Equivalence Class Testing

On the fourth day of his exploration of the Amazon, Byron climbed out of his inner tube, checked the latest news on his personal digital assistant (hereafter PDA) outfitted with wireless technology, and realized that the gnawing he felt in his stomach was not fear—no, he was not afraid, rather elated—nor was it tension—no, he was actually rather relaxed—so it was in all probability a parasite.

— Chuck Keelan

Introduction

Equivalence class testing is a technique used to reduce the number of test cases to a manageable level while still maintaining reasonable test coverage. This simple technique is used intuitively by almost all testers, even though they may not be aware of it as a formal test design method. Many testers have logically deduced its usefulness, while others have discovered it simply because of lack of time to test more thoroughly.

Consider this situation. We are writing a module for a human resources system that decides how we should process employment applications based on a person's age. Our organization's rules are:

0-16	Don't hire
16-18	Can hire on a part-time basis only
18-55	Can hire as a full-time employee
55-99	Don't hire*

Should we test the module for the following ages: 0, 1, 2, 3, 4, 5, 6, 7, 8, …, 90, 91, 92, 93, 94, 95, 96, 97, 98, 99? If we had lots of time (and didn't mind the mind-numbing repetition and were being paid by the hour) we certainly could. If the programmer had implemented this module with the following code we should test each age. (If you don't have a programming background don't worry. These examples are simple. Just read the code and it will make sense to you.)

```
If (applicantAge == 0) hireStatus="NO";
If (applicantAge == 1) hireStatus="NO";
...
```

■■■■■■■■■■■■■■■■■

Observation

With these rules our organization would not have hired Doogie Houser, M.D. or Col. Harlan Sanders, one too young, the other too old.

---

* Note: If you've spotted a problem with these requirements, don't worry. They are written this way for a purpose and will be repaired in the next chapter.

```
If (applicantAge == 14) hireStatus="NO";
If (applicantAge == 15) hireStatus="NO";
If (applicantAge == 16) hireStatus="PART";
If (applicantAge == 17) hireStatus="PART";
If (applicantAge == 18) hireStatus="FULL";
If (applicantAge == 19) hireStatus="FULL";
...
If (applicantAge == 53) hireStatus="FULL";
If (applicantAge == 54) hireStatus="FULL";
If (applicantAge == 55) hireStatus="NO";
If (applicantAge == 56) hireStatus="NO";
...
If (applicantAge == 98) hireStatus="NO";
If (applicantAge == 99) hireStatus="NO";
```

Given this implementation, the fact that any set of tests passes tells us nothing about the next test we could execute. It may pass; it may fail.

Luckily, programmers don't write code like this (at least not very often). A better programmer might write:

```
If (applicantAge >= 0 && applicantAge <=16)
       hireStatus="NO";
If (applicantAge >= 16 && applicantAge <=18)
       hireStatus="PART";
If (applicantAge >= 18 && applicantAge <=55)
       hireStatus="FULL";
If (applicantAge >= 55 && applicantAge <=99)
       hireStatus="NO";
```

Given this typical implementation, it is clear that for the first requirement we don't have to test 0, 1, 2, ... 14, 15, and 16. Only one value needs to be tested. And which value? Any one within that range is just as good as any other one. The same is true for each of the other ranges. Ranges such as the ones described here are called **equivalence classes**. An equivalence class consists of a set of data that is treated the same by the module or that should produce the same result. Any data value within a class is *equivalent*, in terms of testing, to any other value. Specifically, we would expect that:

- If one test case in an equivalence class detects a defect, *all* other test cases in the same equivalence class are likely to detect the same defect.

- If one test case in an equivalence class does not detect a defect, *no* other test cases in the same equivalence class is likely to detect the defect.

This approach assumes, of course, that a specification exists that defines the various equivalence classes to be tested. It also assumes that the programmer has not done something strange such as:

```
If (applicantAge >= 0 && applicantAge <=16)
        hireStatus="NO";
If (applicantAge >= 16 && applicantAge <=18)
        hireStatus="PART";
If (applicantAge >= 18 && applicantAge <=41)
        hireStatus="FULL";
// strange statements follow
If (applicantAge == 42 && applicantName == "Lee")
        hireStatus="HIRE NOW AT HUGE SALARY";
If (applicantAge == 42 && applicantName <> "Lee")
        hireStatus="FULL";
// end of strange statements

If (applicantAge >= 43 && applicantAge <=55)
        hireStatus="FULL";
If (applicantAge >= 55 && applicantAge <=99)
        hireStatus="NO";
```

Using the equivalence class approach, we have reduced the number of test cases from 100 (testing each age) to four (testing one age in each equivalence class)—a significant savings.

Key Point

A group of tests forms an equivalence class if you believe that:

- They all test the same thing.
- If one test catches a bug, the others probably will too.
- If one test doesn't catch a bug, the others probably won't either.

Cem Kaner
Testing Computer Software

Now, are we ready to begin testing? Probably not. What about input values like 969, -42, FRED, and &$#!@? Should we create test cases for invalid input? The answer is, as any good consultant will tell you, "it depends." To understand this answer we need to examine an approach that came out of the object-oriented world called **design-by-contract.**

In law, a **contract** is a legally binding agreement between two (or more) parties that describes what each party promises to do or not do. Each of these promises is of benefit to the other.

In the design-by-contract approach, modules (called "methods" in the object-oriented paradigm, but "module" is a more generic term) are defined in terms of pre-conditions and post-conditions. Post-conditions define what a module promises to do (compute a value, open a file, print a report, update a database record, change the state of the system, etc.). Pre-conditions define what that module requires so that it can meet its post-conditions. For example, if we had a module called openFile, what does it promise to do? Open a file. What would legitimate pre-conditions of openFile be? First, the file must exist; second, we must provide the name (or other identifying information) of the file; third, the file must be "openable," that is, it cannot already be exclusively opened by another process; fourth, we must have access rights to the file; and so on. Pre-conditions and post-conditions establish a contract between a module and others that invoke it.

Testing-by-contract is based on the design-by-contract philosophy. Its approach is to create test cases only for the situations in which the pre-conditions are met. For example, we would not test the openFile module when the file did not exist. The reason is simple. If the file does not exist, openFile does not promise to work. If there is no claim that it will work under a specific condition, there is no need to test under that condition.

■■■■■■■■■■■■■■■■■
Note

According to the Bible, the age of Methuselah when he died was 969 years (Gen 5:27). Thanks to the Gideons who made this data easily accessible in my hotel room without the need for a high speed Internet connection.

■■■■■■■■■■■■■■■■■
For More Information

See Bertrand Meyer's book *Object-Oriented Software Construction* for more on design-by-contract.

At this point testers usually protest. Yes, they agree, the module does not claim to work in that case, but what if the pre-conditions are violated during production? What does the system do? Do we get a misspelled word on the screen or a smoking crater where our company used to be?

A different approach to design is **defensive design**. In this case the module is designed to accept any input. If the normal pre-conditions are met, the module will achieve its normal post-conditions. If the normal pre-conditions are not met, the module will notify the caller by returning an error code or throwing an exception (depending on the programming language used). This notification is actually another one of the module's post-conditions. Based on this approach we could define **defensive testing:** an approach that tests under both normal and abnormal pre-conditions.

How does this apply to equivalence class testing? Do we have to test with inputs like -42, FRED, and &$#!@? If we are using design-by-contract and testing-by-contract the answer is No. If we are using defensive design and thus defensive testing, the answer is Yes. Ask your designers which approach they are using. If they answer either "contract" or "defensive," you know what style of testing to use. If they answer "Huh?" that means they are not thinking about how modules interface. They are not thinking about pre-condition and post-condition contracts. You should expect integration testing to be a prime source of defects that will be more complex and take more time than anticipated.

Technique

The steps for using equivalence class testing are simple. First, identify the equivalence classes. Second, create a test case for each equivalence class. You could create additional test cases for each equivalence class if you have the time and money. Additional test cases may make you feel warm and fuzzy, but they rarely discover defects the first doesn't find.

Different types of input require different types of equivalence classes. Let's consider four possibilities. Let's assume a defensive testing philosophy of testing both valid and invalid input. Testing invalid inputs is often a great source of defects.

If an input is a continuous range of values, then there is typically one class of valid values and two classes of invalid values, one below the valid class and one above it. Consider the Goofy Mortgage Company (GMC). They will write mortgages for people with incomes between $1,000/month and $83,333/month. Anything below $1,000/month you don't qualify. Anything over $83,333/month you don't need GMC, just pay cash.

For a valid input we might choose $1,342/month. For invalids we might choose $123/month and $90,000/month.

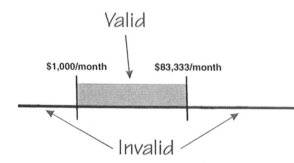

If an input condition takes on discrete values within a range of permissible values, there are typically one valid and two invalid classes. GMC will write a single mortgage for one through five houses. (Remember, it's Goofy.) Zero or fewer houses is not a legitimate input, nor is six or greater. Neither are fractional or decimal values such as 2½ or 3.14159.

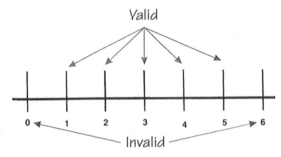

Figure 3-2

Discrete
equivalence classes

For a valid input we might choose two houses. Invalids could be −2 and 8.

GMC will make mortgages only for a person. They will not make mortgages for corporations, trusts, partnerships, or any other type of legal entity.

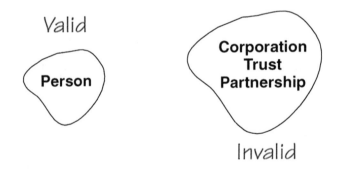

Figure 3-3

Single selection
equivalence classes

For a valid input we *must* use "person." For an invalid we could choose "corporation" or "trust" or any other random text string. How many invalid cases should we create? We must have at least one; we may choose additional tests for additional warm and fuzzy feelings.

GMC will make mortgages on Condominiums, Townhouses, and Single Family dwellings. They will not make mortgages on Duplexes, Mobile Homes, Treehouses, or any other type of dwelling.

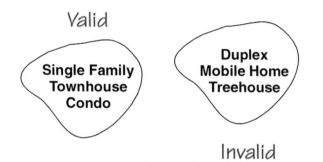

For valid input we must choose from "Condominium," "Townhouse," or "Single Family." While the rule says choose one test case from the valid equivalence class, a more comprehensive approach would be to create test cases for each entry in the valid class. That makes sense when the list of valid values is small. But, if this were a list of the fifty states, the District of Columbia, and the various territories of the United States, would you test every one of them? What if the list were every country in the world? The correct answer, of course, depends on the risk to the organization if, as testers, we miss something that is vital.

Now, rarely will we have the time to create individual tests for every separate equivalence class of every input value that enters our system. More often, we will create test cases that test a number of input fields simultaneously. For example, we might create a *single* test case with the following combination of inputs:

Monthly Income	Number of Dwellings	Applicant	Dwelling Types	Result
$5,000	2	Person	Condo	Valid

Each of these data values is in the valid range, so we would expect the system to perform correctly and for the test case to report Pass.

It is tempting to use the same approach for invalid values.

Monthly Income	Number of Dwellings	Applicant	Dwelling Types	Result
$100	8	Partnership	Treehouse	Invalid

If the system accepts this input as valid, clearly the system is not validating the four input fields properly. If the system rejects this input as invalid, it may do so in such a way that the tester cannot determine which field it rejected. For example:

ERROR: 653X-2.7 INVALID INPUT

In many cases, errors in one input field may cancel out or mask errors in another field so the system accepts the data as valid. A better approach is to test one invalid value at a time to verify the system detects it correctly.

Monthly Income	Number of Dwellings	Applicant	Dwelling Types	Result
$100	1	Person	SingleFam	Invalid
$1,342	**0**	Person	Condo	Invalid
$1,342	1	**Corporation**	Townhouse	Invalid
$1,342	1	Person	**Treehouse**	Invalid

For additional warm and fuzzy feelings, the inputs (both valid and invalid) could be varied.

Monthly Income	Number of Dwellings	Applicant	Dwelling Types	Result
$100	1	Person	Single Family	Invalid
$1,342	**0**	Person	Condominium	Invalid
$5,432	3	**Corporation**	Townhouse	Invalid
$10,000	2	Person	**Treehouse**	Invalid

Another approach to using equivalence classes is to examine the outputs rather than the inputs. Divide the outputs into equivalence classes, then determine what input values would cause those outputs. This has the advantage of guiding the tester to examine, and thus test, every different kind of output. But this approach can be deceiving. In the previous example, for the human resources system, one of the system outputs was NO, that is, Don't Hire. A cursory view of the inputs that should cause this output would yield {0, 1, ..., 14, 15}. Note that this is *not* the complete set. In addition {55, 56, ..., 98, 99} should also cause the NO output. It's important to make sure that all potential outputs can be generated, but don't be fooled into choosing equivalence class data that omits important inputs.

Examples

Example 1

Referring to the **Trade** Web page of the Brown & Donaldson Web site described in Appendix A, consider the **Order Type** field. The designer has chosen to implement the decision to Buy or Sell through radio buttons. This is a good design choice because it reduces the number of test cases the tester must create. Had this been implemented as a text field in which the user entered "Buy" or "Sell" the tester would have partitioned the valid inputs as {Buy, Sell} and the invalids as {Trade, Punt, ...}. What about "buy", "bUy", "BUY"? Are these valid or invalid entries? The tester would have to refer back to the requirements to determine their status.

With the radio button implementation no invalid choices exist, so none need to be tested. Only the valid inputs {Buy, Sell} need to be exercised.

■■■■■■■■■■■■■■■■■■
Insight

Let your designers and programmers know when they have helped you. They'll appreciate the thought and may do it again.

Example 2

Again, referring to the **Trade** Web page, consider the **Quantity** field. Input to this field can be between one and four numeric characters (0,1, …, 8,9) with a valid value greater or equal to 1 and less than or equal to 9999. A set of valid inputs is {1, 22, 333, 4444} while invalid inputs are {-42, 0, 12345, SQE, $#@%}.

Example 3

On the **Trade** page the user enters a ticker **Symbol** indicating the stock to buy or sell. The valid symbols are {A, AA, AABC, AAC, …, ZOLT, ZOMX, ZONA, ZRAN}. The invalid symbols are any combination of characters not included in the valid list. A set of valid inputs could be {A, AL, ABE, ACES, AKZOY} while a set of invalids could be {C, AF, BOB, CLUBS, AKZAM, 42, @#$%}.

Example 4

Rarely will we create separate sets of test cases for each input. Generally it is more efficient to test multiple inputs simultaneously within tests. For example, the following tests combine Buy/Sell, Symbol, and Quantity.

Buy/Sell	Symbol	Quantity	Result
Buy	A	10	Valid
Buy	C	20	Invalid
Buy	A	0	Invalid
Sell	ACES	10	Valid
Sell	**BOB**	33	Invalid
Sell	ABE	**-3**	Invalid

■■■■■■■■■■■■■■■■■
Insight

Very often your designers and programmers use GUI design tools that can enforce restrictions on the length and content of input fields. Encourage their use. Then your testing can focus on making sure the requirement has been implemented properly with the tool.

■■■■■■■■■■■■■■■■■
For More Information

Click on the **Symbol Lookup** button on the B&D Trade page to see the full list of stock symbols.

■■■■■■■■■■■■■■■■■
Table 3-5

A set of test cases varying invalid values one by one.

Applicability and Limitations

Equivalence class testing can significantly reduce the number of test cases that must be created and executed. It is most suited to systems in which much of the input data takes on values within ranges or within sets. It makes the assumption that data in the same equivalence class is, in fact, processed in the same way by the system. The simplest way to validate this assumption is to ask the programmer about their implementation.

Equivalence class testing is equally applicable at the unit, integration, system, and acceptance test levels. All it requires are inputs or outputs that can be partitioned based on the system's requirements.

Summary

- Equivalence class testing is a technique used to reduce the number of test cases to a manageable size while still maintaining reasonable coverage.

- This simple technique is used intuitively by almost all testers, even though they may not be aware of it as a formal test design method.

- An equivalence class consists of a set of data that is treated the same by the module or that should produce the same result. Any data value within a class is equivalent, in terms of testing, to any other value.

Practice

1. The following exercises refer to the Stateless University Registration System Web site described in Appendix B. Define the equivalence classes and suitable test cases for the following:

   a. ZIP Code—five numeric digits.

   b. State—the standard Post Office two-character abbreviation for the states, districts, territories, etc. of the United States.

   c. Last Name—one through fifteen characters (including alphabetic characters, periods, hyphens, apostrophes, spaces, and numbers).

   d. User ID—eight characters at least two of which are not alphabetic (numeric, special, nonprinting).

   e. Student ID—eight characters. The first two represent the student's home campus while the last six are a unique six-digit number. Valid home campus abbreviations are: AN, Annandale; LC, Las Cruces; RW, Riverside West; SM, San Mateo; TA, Talbot; WE, Weber; and WN, Wenatchee.

References

Beizer, Boris (1990). *Software Testing Techniques*. Van Nostrand Reinhold.

Kaner, Cem, Jack Falk and Hung Quoc Nguyen (1999). *Testing Computer Software* (Second Edition). John Wiley & Sons.

Myers, Glenford J. (1979). *The Art of Software Testing*. John Wiley & Sons.

Chapter 4 –
Boundary Value Testing

The Prince looked down at the motionless form of Sleeping Beauty, wondering how her supple lips would feel against his own and contemplating whether or not an Altoid was strong enough to stand up against the kind of morning breath only a hundred years' nap could create.

— Lynne Sella

Introduction

Equivalence class testing is the most basic test design technique. It helps testers choose a small subset of possible test cases while maintaining reasonable coverage. Equivalence class testing has a second benefit. It leads us to the idea of boundary value testing, the second key test design technique to be presented.

In the previous chapter the following rules were given that indicate how we should process employment applications based on a person's age. The rules were:

0-16	Don't hire
16-18	Can hire on a part-time basis only
18-55	Can hire as a full-time employee
55-99	Don't hire

Notice the problem at the boundaries—the "edges" of each class. The age "16" is included in two different equivalence classes (as are 18 and 55). The first rule says don't hire a 16-year-old. The second rule says a 16-year-old can be hired on a part-time basis.

Boundary value testing focuses on the boundaries simply because that is where so many defects hide. Experienced testers have encountered this situation many times. Inexperienced testers may have an intuitive feel that mistakes will occur most often at the boundaries. These defects can be in the requirements (as shown above) or in the code as shown below:

■■■■■■■■■■■■■■■■■
Key Point

Boundary value testing focuses on the boundaries because that is where so many defects hide.

```
If (applicantAge >= 0 && applicantAge <=16)
        hireStatus="NO";
If (applicantAge >= 16 && applicantAge <=18)
        hireStatus="PART";
If (applicantAge >= 18 && applicantAge <=55)
        hireStatus="FULL";
If (applicantAge >= 55 && applicantAge <=99)
        hireStatus="NO";
```

Of course, the mistake that programmers make is coding inequality tests improperly. Writing > (greater than) instead of ≥ (greater than or equal) is an example.

The most efficient way of finding such defects, either in the requirements or the code, is through inspection. Gilb and Graham's book, *Software Inspection*, is an excellent guide to this process. However, no matter how effective our inspections, we will want to test the code to verify its correctness.

Perhaps this is what our organization meant:

    0-15   Don't hire
    16-17 Can hire on a part-time basis only
    18-54 Can hire as full-time employees
    55-99 Don't hire

What about ages –3 and 101? Note that the requirements do not specify how these values should be treated. We could guess but "guessing the requirements" is not an acceptable practice.

The code that implements the corrected rules is:

```
If (applicantAge >= 0 && applicantAge <=15)
        hireStatus="NO";
If (applicantAge >= 16 && applicantAge <=17)
        hireStatus="PART";
```

```
If (applicantAge >= 18 && applicantAge <=54)
        hireStatus="FULL";
If (applicantAge >= 55 && applicantAge <=99)
        hireStatus="NO";
```

The interesting values on or near the boundaries in this example are {-1, 0, 1}, {15, 16, 17}, {17, 18, 19}, {54, 55, 56}, and {98, 99, 100}. Other values, such as {-42, 1001, FRED, %$#@} might be included depending on the module's documented pre-conditions.

Technique

The steps for using boundary value testing are simple. First, identify the equivalence classes. Second, identify the boundaries of each equivalence class. Third, create test cases for each boundary value by choosing one point on the boundary, one point just below the boundary, and one point just above the boundary. "Below" and "above" are relative terms and depend on the data value's units. If the boundary is 16 and the unit is "integer" then the "below" point is 15 and the "above" point is 17. If the boundary is $5.00 and the unit is "US dollars and cents" then the below point is $4.99 and the above point is $5.01. On the other hand, if the value is $5 and the unit is "US dollars" then the below point is $4 and the above point is $6.

Note that a point just above one boundary may be in another equivalence class. There is no reason to duplicate the test. The same may be true of the point just below the boundary.

You could, of course, create additional test cases farther from the boundaries (within equivalence classes) if you have the resources. As discussed in the previous chapter, these additional test cases may make you feel warm and fuzzy, but they rarely discover additional defects.

■■■■■■■■■■■■■■■■■■

Key Point

Create test cases for each boundary value by choosing one point on the boundary, one point just below the boundary, and one point just above the boundary.

Boundary value testing is most appropriate where the input is a continuous range of values. Returning again to the Goofy Mortgage Company, what are the interesting boundary values? For monthly income the boundaries are $1,000/month and $83,333/month (assuming the units to be US dollars).

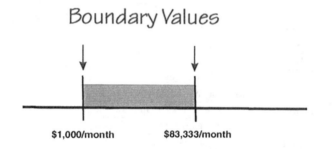

Boundary Values

$1,000/month $83,333/month

Figure 4-1

Boundary values for a continuous range of inputs.

Test data input of {$999, $1,000, $1,001) on the low end and {$83,332, $83,333, $83,334} on the high end are chosen to test the boundaries.

Because GMC will write a mortgage for one through five houses, zero or fewer houses is not a legitimate input nor is six or greater. These identify the boundaries for testing.

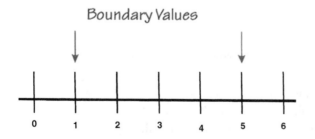

Boundary Values

0   1   2   3   4   5   6

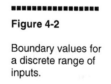

Figure 4-2

Boundary values for a discrete range of inputs.

Rarely will we have the time to create individual tests for every boundary value of every input value that enters our system. More often, we will create test cases that test a number of input fields simultaneously.

Monthly Income	Number of Dwellings	Result	Description
$1,000	1	Valid	Min income, min dwellings
$83,333	1	Valid	Max income, min dwellings
$1,000	5	Valid	Min income, max dwellings
$83,333	5	Valid	Max income, max dwellings
$1,000	0	Invalid	Min income, below min dwellings
$1,000	6	Invalid	Min income, above max dwellings
$83,333	0	Invalid	Max income, below min dwellings
$83,333	6	Invalid	Max income, above max dwellings
$999	1	Invalid	Below min income, min dwellings
$83,334	1	Invalid	Above max income, min dwellings
$999	5	Invalid	Below min income, max dwellings
$83,334	5	Invalid	Above max income, max dwellings

Table 4-1

A set of test cases containing combinations of valid (on the boundary) values and invalid (off the boundary) points.

Plotting "monthly income" on the x-axis and "number of dwellings" on the y-axis shows the "locations" of the test data points.

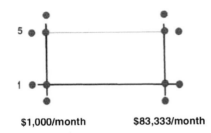

$1,000/month $83,333/month

Figure 4-3

Data points on the boundaries and data points just outside the boundaries.

Note that four of the input combinations are on the boundaries while eight are just outside. Also note that the points outside always combine one valid value with one invalid value (just one unit lower or one unit higher).

Examples

Boundary value testing is applicable to the structure (length and character type) of input data as well as its value. Consider the following two examples:

Example 1

Referring to the **Trade** Web page of the Brown & Donaldson Web site described in Appendix A, consider the **Quantity** field. Input to this field can be between one and four numeric characters (0,1, ..., 8,9). A set of boundary value test cases for the length attribute would be {0, 1, 4, 5} numeric characters.

Example 2

Again, on the **Trade** page, consider the **Quantity** field, but this time for value rather than structure (length and character type). Whether the transaction is Buy or Sell, the minimum legitimate value is 1 so use {0, 1, 2} for boundary testing. The upper limit on this field's value is more complicated. If the transaction is Sell, what is the maximum number of shares that can be sold? It is the number currently owned. For this boundary use {sharesOwned-1, sharesOwned, sharesOwned+1}. If the transaction is Buy, the maximum value (number of shares to be purchased) is defined as

$$shares = (accountBalance - commission) / sharePrice$$

assuming a fixed commission. Use {shares-1, shares, shares+1} as the boundary value test cases.

Applicability and Limitations

Boundary value testing can significantly reduce the number of test cases that must be created and executed. It is most suited to systems in which much of the input data takes on values within ranges or within sets.

Boundary value testing is equally applicable at the unit, integration, system, and acceptance test levels. All it requires are inputs that can be partitioned and boundaries that can be identified based on the system's requirements.

Summary

- While equivalence class testing is useful, its greatest contribution is to lead us to boundary value testing.

- Boundary value testing is a technique used to reduce the number of test cases to a manageable size while still maintaining reasonable coverage.

- Boundary value testing focuses on the boundaries because that is where so many defects hide. Experienced testers have encountered this situation many times. Inexperienced testers may have an intuitive feel that mistakes will occur most often at the boundaries.

- Create test cases for each boundary value by choosing one point on the boundary, one point just below the boundary, and one point just above the boundary. "Below" and "above" are relative terms and depend on the data value's units.

Practice

1. The following exercises refer to the Stateless University Registration System Web site described in Appendix B. Define the boundaries, and suitable boundary value test cases for the following:

    a. ZIP Code—five numeric digits.

    b. First consider ZIP Code just in terms of digits. Then, determine the lowest and highest legitimate ZIP Codes in the United States. For extra credit[*], determine the format of postal codes for Canada and the lowest and highest valid values.

    c. Last Name—one through fifteen characters (including alphabetic characters, periods, hyphens, apostrophes, spaces, and numbers). For extra credit[*] create a few very complex Last Names. Can you determine the "rules" for legitimate Last Names? For additional extra credit[*] use a phonebook from another country—try Finland or Thailand.

    d. User ID—eight characters at least two of which are not alphabetic (numeric, special, nonprinting).

    e. Course ID—three alpha characters representing the department followed by a six-digit integer which is the unique course identification number. The possible departments are:

---

[*] There actually is no extra credit, so do it for fun.

PHY – Physics
EGR – Engineering
ENG – English
LAN – Foreign languages
CHM – Chemistry
MAT – Mathematics
PED – Physical education
SOC – Sociology

References

Beizer, Boris (1990). *Software Testing Techniques*. Van Nostrand Reinhold.

Gilb, Tom and Dorothy Graham (1993). *Software Inspection*. Addison-Wesley. ISBN 0-201-63181-4.

Myers, Glenford J. (1979). *The Art of Software Testing*. John Wiley & Sons.

Chapter 5 –
Decision Table Testing

I'd stumbled onto solving my first murder case, having found myself the only eyewitness, yet no matter how frantically I pleaded with John Law that the perp was right in front of them and the very dame they'd been grilling - the sultry but devious Miss Kitwinkle, who played the grieving patsy the way a concert pianist player plays a piano - the cops just kept smiling and stuffing crackers in my beak.

— Chris Esco

Introduction

Decision tables are an excellent tool to capture certain kinds of system requirements and to document internal system design. They are used to record complex business rules that a system must implement. In addition, they can serve as a guide to creating test cases.

Decision tables are a vital tool in the tester's personal toolbox. Unfortunately, many analysts, designers, programmers, and testers are not familiar with this technique.

Technique

Decision tables represent complex business rules based on a set of conditions. The general form is:

	Rule 1	Rule 2	...	Rule p
Conditions				
Condition-1				
Condition-2				
...				
Condition-m				
Actions				
Action-1				
Action-2				
...				
Action-n				

■■■■■■■■■■■■■■■■■

Table 5-1

The general form of a decision table.

Conditions 1 through m represent various input conditions. Actions 1 through n are the actions that should be taken depending on the various combinations of input conditions. Each of the rules defines a unique combination of conditions that result in the execution ("firing") of the actions associated with that rule. Note that the actions do not depend on the order in which the conditions are evaluated, but only on their values. (All values are assumed to be available simultaneously.) Also, actions depend only on the specified conditions, not on any previous input conditions or system state.

Perhaps a concrete example will clarify the concepts. An auto insurance company gives discounts to drivers who are married and/or good students. Let's begin with the conditions. The following decision table has two conditions, each one of which takes on the values Yes or No.

	Rule 1	Rule 2	Rule 3	Rule 4
Conditions				
Married?	Yes	Yes	No	No
Good Student?	Yes	No	Yes	No

■■■■■■■■■■■■■■■■■■
Table 5-2

A decision table with two binary conditions.

Note that the table contains all combinations of the conditions. Given two binary conditions (Yes or No), the possible combinations are {Yes, Yes}, {Yes, No}, {No, Yes}, and {No, No}. Each rule represents one of these combinations. As a tester we will verify that all combinations of the conditions are defined. Missing a combination may result in developing a system that may not process a particular set of inputs properly.

Now for the actions. Each rule causes an action to "fire." Each rule may specify an action unique to that rule, or rules may share actions.

	Rule 1	Rule 2	Rule 3	Rule 4
Conditions				
Married?	Yes	Yes	No	No
Good Student?	Yes	No	Yes	No
Actions				
Discount ($)	60	25	50	0

■■■■■■■■■■■■■■■■■

Table 5-3

Adding a single
action to a decision
table.
_____

Decision tables may specify more than one action for each rule. Again, these rules may be unique or may be shared.

	Rule 1	Rule 2	Rule 3	Rule 4
Conditions				
Condition-1	Yes	Yes	No	No
Condition-2	Yes	No	Yes	No
Actions				
Action-1	Do X	Do Y	Do X	Do Z
Action-2	Do A	Do B	Do B	Do B

■■■■■■■■■■■■■■■■■

Table 5-4

A decision table
with multiple
actions.
_____

In this situation, choosing test cases is simple—each rule (vertical column) becomes a test case. The Conditions specify the inputs and the Actions specify the expected results.

While the previous example uses simple binary conditions, conditions can be more complex.

	Rule 1	Rule 2	Rule 3	Rule 4
Conditions				
Condition-1	0-1	1-10	10-100	100-1000
Condition-2	<5	5	6 or 7	>7
Actions				
Action-1	Do X	Do Y	Do X	Do Z
Action-2	Do A	Do B	Do B	Do B

■■■■■■■■■■■■■■■■■

Table 5-5

A decision table
with non-binary
conditions.
_____

In this situation choosing test cases is slightly more complex—each rule (vertical column) becomes a test case but values satisfying the conditions must be chosen. Choosing appropriate values we create the following test cases:

Test Case ID	Condition-1	Condition-2	Expected Result
TC1	0	3	Do X / Do A
TC2	5	5	Do Y / Do B
TC3	50	7	Do X / Do B
TC4	500	10	Do Z / Do B

■■■■■■■■■■■■■■■■■■
Table 5-6

Sample test cases.
_____

If the system under test has complex business rules, and if your business analysts or designers have not documented these rules in this form, testers should gather this information and represent it in decision table form. The reason is simple. Given the system behavior represented in this complete and compact form, test cases can be created directly from the decision table.

In testing, create at least one test case for each rule. If the rule's conditions are binary, a single test for each combination is probably sufficient. On the other hand, if a condition is a range of values, consider testing at both the low and high end of the range. In this way we merge the ideas of Boundary Value testing with Decision Table testing.

■■■■■■■■■■■■■■■■■■
Key Point

Create at least one test case for each rule.
_____

To create a test case table simply change the row and column headings:

	Test Case 1	Test Case 2	Test Case 3	Test Case 4
Inputs				
Condition-1	Yes	Yes	No	No
Condition-2	Yes	No	Yes	No
Expected Results				
Action-1	Do X	Do Y	Do X	Do Z
Action-2	Do A	Do B	Do B	Do B

Table 5-7

A decision table converted to a test case table.

Examples

Decision Table testing can be used whenever the system must implement complex business rules. Consider the following two examples:

Example 1

Table 5-8

A decision table for the Brown & Donaldson Buy order.

Referring to the **Trade** Web page of the Brown & Donaldson Web site described in Appendix A, consider the rules associated with a **Buy** order.

	Rule 1	Rule 2	Rule 3	Rule 4	Rule 5	Rule 6	Rule 7	Rule 8
Conditions								
Valid Symbol	No	No	No	No	Yes	Yes	Yes	Yes
Valid Quantity	No	No	Yes	Yes	No	No	Yes	Yes
Sufficient Funds	No	Yes	No	Yes	No	Yes	No	Yes
Actions								
Buy?	No	No	No	No	No	No	No	Yes

Admittedly, the outcome is readily apparent. Only when a valid symbol, valid quantity, and sufficient funds are available should the **Buy** order be placed. This example was chosen to illustrate another concept.

Examine the first four columns. If the **Symbol** is not valid, none of the other conditions matter. Often tables like this are collapsed, rules are combined, and the conditions that do not affect the outcome are marked "DC" for "Don't Care." Rule 1 now indicates that if the **Symbol** is not valid, ignore the other conditions and do not execute the **Buy** order.

	Rule 1	**Rule 2**	**Rule 3**	**Rule 4**	**Rule 5**
Conditions					
Valid Symbol	No	Yes	Yes	Yes	Yes
Valid Quantity	DC	No	No	Yes	Yes
Sufficient Funds	DC	No	Yes	No	Yes
Actions					
Buy?	No	No	No	No	Yes

Table 5-9

A collapsed decision table reflecting "Don't Care" conditions.

Note also that Rule 2 and Rule 3 can be combined because whether Sufficient Funds are available does not affect the action.

	Rule 1	**Rule 2**	**Rule 3**	**Rule 4**
Conditions				
Valid Symbol	No	Yes	Yes	Yes
Valid Quantity	DC	No	Yes	Yes
Sufficient Funds	DC	DC	No	Yes
Actions				
Buy?	No	No	No	Yes

Table 5-10

A further collapsed decision table reflecting "Don't Care" conditions.

While this is an excellent idea from a development standpoint because less code is written, it is dangerous from a testing standpoint. It is always possible that the table was collapsed incorrectly or the code was written improperly. The un-collapsed table should always be used as the basis for our test case design.

Example 2

The following screen is from the Stateless University Registration System. It is used to enter new students into the system, to modify student information, and to delete students from the system.

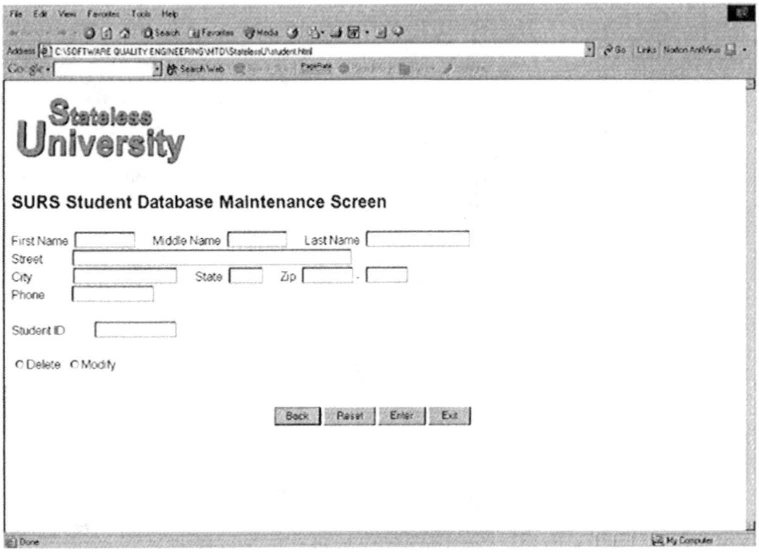

■■■■■■■■■■■■■■■■■

Figure 5-1

SURS Student
Database
Maintenance
Screen.

To enter a new student, enter name, address, and telephone information on the upper part of the screen and press Enter. The student is entered into the database and the system returns a new StudentID. To modify or delete a student, enter the StudentID, select the Delete or Modify radio button and press Enter. The decision table reflecting these rules follows:

	Rule 1	Rule 2	Rule 3	Rule 4	Rule 5	Rule 6	Rule 7	Rule 8
Conditions								
Entered Student data	No	No	No	No	No	No	No	No
Entered Student ID	No	No	No	No	Yes	Yes	Yes	Yes
Selected Modify	No	No	Yes	Yes	No	No	Yes	Yes
Selected Delete	No	Yes	No	Yes	No	Yes	No	Yes
Actions								
Create new student	No	No	No	No	No	No	No	No
Modify Student	No	No	No	No	No	No	Yes	No
Delete Student	No	No	No	No	No	Yes	No	No

Table 5-11

A decision table for Stateless University Registration System.

	Rule 9	Rule 10	Rule 11	Rule 12	Rule 13	Rule 14	Rule 15	Rule 16
Conditions								
Entered Student data	Yes	Yes	Yes	Yes	Yes	Yes	Yes	Yes
Entered Student ID	No	No	No	No	Yes	Yes	Yes	Yes
Selected Modify	No	No	Yes	Yes	No	No	Yes	Yes
Selected Delete	No	Yes	No	Yes	No	Yes	No	Yes
Actions								
Create new student	Yes	No	No	No	No	No	No	No
Modify Student	No	No	Yes	No	No	No	No	No
Delete Student	No	No	No	No	No	No	No	No

Rules 1 through 8 indicate that no data was entered about the student. Rules 1 through 4 indicate that no StudentID was entered for the student, thus no action is possible. Rules 5 through 8 indicate the StudentID was entered. In these cases creating a new Student is not proper. Rule 5 does not request either modification or deletion so neither is done. Rules 6 and 7 request one function and so they are performed. Note that Rule 8 indicates that both modification and deletion are to be performed so no action is taken.

Rules 9 through 16 indicate that data was entered about the student. Rules 9 through 12 indicate that no StudentID was entered so these rules refer to a new student. Rule 9 creates a new student. Rule 10 deletes the student. Rule 11 allows modification of the student's data. Rule 12 requests that both modification and deletion are to be performed so no action is taken. Rules 13 through 16 supply student data indicating a new student but also provide a StudentID indicating an existing student. Because of this contradictory input, no action is taken. Often, error messages are displayed in these situations.

Applicability and Limitations

Decision Table testing can be used whenever the system must implement complex business rules when these rules can be represented as a combination of conditions and when these conditions have discrete actions associated with them.

Summary

- Decision tables are used to document complex business rules that a system must implement. In addition, they serve as a guide to creating test cases.

- Conditions represent various input conditions. Actions are the processes that should be executed depending on the various combinations of input conditions. Each rule defines a unique combination of conditions that result in the execution ("firing") of the actions associated with that rule.

- Create at least one test case for each rule. If the rule's conditions are binary, a single test for each combination is probably sufficient. On the other hand, if a condition is a range of values, consider testing at both the low and high end of the range.

Practice

1. Attending Stateless University is an expensive proposition. After all, they receive no state funding. Like many other students, those planning on attending apply for student aid using FAFSA, the Free Application for Federal Student Aid. The following instructions were taken from that form. Examine them and create a decision table that represents the FAFSA rules. (Note: You can't make up stuff like this.)

   Step Four: Who is considered a parent in this step?

Read these notes to determine who is considered a parent for purposes of this form. **Answer all questions in Step Four about them**, even if you do not live with them.

Are you an orphan, or are you or were you (until age 18) a ward/dependent of the court? If Yes, skip Step Four. If your parents are both living and married to each other, answer the questions about them. If your parent is widowed or single, answer the questions about that parent. If your widowed parent is remarried as of today, answer the questions about that parent **and** the person whom your parent married (your stepparent). If your parents are divorced or separated, answer the questions about the parent you lived with more during the past 12 months. (If you did not live with one parent more than the other, give answers about the parent who provided more financial support during the last 12 months, or during the most recent year that you actually received support from a parent.) If this parent is remarried as of today, answer the questions on the rest of this form about that parent **and** the person whom your parent married (your stepparent).

References

Beizer, Boris (1990). *Software Testing Techniques* (Second Edition). Van Nostrand Reinhold.

Binder, Robert V. (2000). *Testing Object-Oriented Systems: Models, Patterns, and Tools*. Addison-Wesley.

Chapter 6 –
Pairwise Testing

Anton was attracted to Angela like a moth to a flame - not just any moth, but one of the giant silk moths of the genus Hyalophora, perhaps Hyalophora euryalus, whose great red-brown wings with white basal and postmedian lines flap almost languorously until one ignites in the flame, fanning the conflagration to ever greater heights until burning down to the hirsute thorax and abdomen, the fat-laden contents of which provide a satisfying sizzle to end the agony.

— Andrew Amlen

Introduction

A s they used to say on *Monty Python*, "And now for something completely different."

Consider these situations:

- A Web site must operate correctly with different browsers—Internet Explorer 5.0, 5.5, and 6.0, Netscape 6.0, 6.1, and 7.0, Mozilla 1.1, and Opera 7; using different plug-ins—RealPlayer, MediaPlayer, or none; running on different client operating systems—Windows 95, 98, ME, NT, 2000, and XP; receiving pages from different servers—IIS, Apache, and WebLogic; running on different server operating systems—Windows NT, 2000, and Linux.

  Web Combinations

  8 browsers
  3 plug-ins
  6 client operating systems
  3 servers
  3 server OS

  1,296 combinations.

- A bank has created a new data processing system that is ready for testing. This bank has different kinds of customers—consumers, very important consumers, businesses, and non-profits; different kinds of accounts—checking, savings, mortgages, consumer loans, and commercial loans; they operate in different states, each with different regulations—California, Nevada, Utah, Idaho, Arizona, and New Mexico.

  Bank Combinations

  4 customer types
  5 account types
  6 states

  120 combinations.

- In an object-oriented system, an object of class A can pass a message containing a parameter P to an object of class X. Classes B, C, and D inherit from A so they too can send the message. Classes Q, R, S, and T inherit from P so they too can be passed as the parameter. Classes Y and Z inherit from X so they too can receive the message.

  OO Combinations
  4 senders
  5 parameters
  3 receivers

  60 combinations.

What do these very different situations all have in common? Each has a large number of combinations that should be tested. Each has a large number of combinations that may be risky if we do not test. Each has such a large number of combinations that we may not have the resources to construct and run all the tests, there are just too many. We must, somehow, select a reasonably sized subset that we could test given our resource constraints. What are some ways of choosing such a subset? This list starts with the worst schemes but does improve:

Worst

- Don't test at all. Simply give up because the number of input combinations, and thus the number of test cases, is just too great.

- Test all combinations [once], but delay the project so it misses its market window so that everyone quits from stress, or the company goes out of business.

- Choose one or two tests and hope for the best.

- Choose the tests that you have already run, perhaps as part of programmer-led testing. Incorporate them into a formal test plan and run them again.

- Choose the tests that are easy to create and run. Ignore whether they provide useful information about the quality of the product.

- Make a list of all the combinations and choose the first few.

- Make a list of all the combinations and choose a random subset.

■■■■■■■■■■■■■■■■■■
Insight

Students in my classes often have a very difficult time thinking of bad ways to do things. Cultivate the skill of choosing poorly. It will be invaluable in evaluating others' ideas.

■■■■■■■■■■■■■■■■■■
Can You Believe This?

A student in one of my classes shared this story: His organization uses a process they call "Post-Installation Test Planning." It sounds impressive until you decipher it. Whatever tests they happen to run that happen to pass are documented as their Test Plan.

Best ⬇

- By magic, choose a specially selected, fairly small subset that finds a great many defects—more than you would expect from such a subset.

This last scheme sounds like a winner (but it is a little vague). The question is—what is the "magic" that allows us to choose that "specially selected" subset?

The answer is not to attempt to test all the combinations for all the values for all the variables but to test **all pairs** of variables. This significantly reduces the number of tests that must be created and run. Consider the significant reductions in test effort in these examples:

- If a system had four different input parameters and each one could take on one of three different values, the number of combinations is 3^4 which is 81. It is possible to cover all the pairwise input combinations in only nine tests.

- If a system had thirteen different input parameters and each one could take on one of three different values, the number of combinations is 3^{13} which is 1,594,323. It is possible to cover all the pairwise input combinations in only fifteen tests.

- If a system had twenty different input parameters and each one could take on one of ten different values, the number of combinations is 10^{20}. It is possible to cover all the pairwise input combinations in only 180 tests.

There is much anecdotal evidence about the benefit of pairwise testing. Unfortunately, there are only a few documented studies:

- In a case study published by Brownlie of AT&T regarding the testing of a local-area network-based

■■■■■■■■■■■■■■■■■
Insight

Random selection can be a very good approach to choosing a subset but most people have a difficult time choosing truly randomly.

────────────

electronic mail system, pairwise testing detected 28 percent more defects than their original plan of developing and executing 1,500 test cases (later reduced to 1,000 because of time constraints) and took 50 percent less effort.

- A study by the National Institute of Standards and Technology published by Wallace and Kuhn on software defects in recalled medical devices reviewed fifteen years of defect data. They concluded that 98 percent of the reported software flaws could have been detected by testing all pairs of parameter settings.

- Kuhn and Reilly analyzed defects recorded in the Mozilla Web browser database. They determined that pairwise testing would have detected 76 percent of the reported errors.

Why does pairwise testing work so well? I don't know. There is no underlying "software physics" that requires it. One hypothesis is that most defects are either single-mode defects (the function under test simply does not work and any test of that function would find the defect) or they are double-mode defects (it is the pairing of this function/module with that function/module that fails even though all other pairings perform properly). Pairwise testing defines a minimal subset that guides us to test for all single-mode and double-mode defects. The success of this technique on many projects, both documented and undocumented, is a great motivation for its use.

■■■■■■■■■■■■■■■■■■
Note

Pairwise testing may not choose combinations which the developers and testers know are either frequently used or highly risky. If these combinations exist, use the pairwise tests, then add additional test cases to minimize the risk of missing an important combination.

Technique

Two different techniques are used to identify all the pairs for creating test cases—orthogonal arrays and the Allpairs algorithm.

Orthogonal Arrays

What are orthogonal arrays? The origin of orthogonal arrays can be traced back to Euler, the great mathematician, in the guise of Latin Squares. Genichi Taguchi has popularized their use in hardware testing. An excellent reference book is *Quality Engineering Using Robust Design* by Madhav S. Phadke.

Consider the numbers 1 and 2. How many pair combinations (combinations taken two at a time) of '1' and '2' exist? {1,1}, {1,2}, {2,1} and {2,2}. An orthogonal array is a two-dimensional array of numbers that has this interesting property—choose any two columns in the array. All the pairwise combinations of its values will occur in every pair of columns. Let's examine an $L_4(2^3)$ array:

	1	2	3
1	1	1	1
2	1	2	2
3	2	1	2
4	2	2	1

Table 6-1

$L_4(2^3)$ Orthogonal Array

The gray column headings and row numbers are not part of the orthogonal array but are included for convenience in referencing the cells. Examine columns 1 and 2—do the four combinations of 1 and 2 all appear in that column pair? Yes, and in the order listed earlier. Now examine columns 1 and 3—do the four combinations of 1 and 2 appear in that column pair? Yes, although in a different order. Finally, examine columns 2 and 3—do the four combinations appear in that column pair also? Yes they do. The $L_4(2^3)$ array is orthogonal; that is, choose any two columns, all the pairwise combinations will occur in all the column pairs.

A note about the curious (but standard) notation: L_4 means an orthogonal array with four rows, (2^3) is not an exponent. It means that the array has three columns, each with either a 1 or a 2.

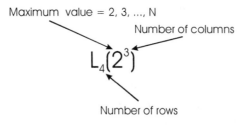

Figure 6-1

Orthogonal array notation

Let's consider a larger orthogonal array. Given the numbers 1, 2 and 3, how many pair combinations of 1, 2, and 3 exist? {1,1}, {1,2}, {1,3}, {2,1}, {2,2}, {2,3}, {3,1}, {3,2}, and {3,3}. Below is an $L_9(3^4)$ array:

	1	2	3	4
1	1	1	1	1
2	1	2	2	2
3	1	3	3	3
4	2	1	2	3
5	2	2	3	1
6	2	3	1	2
7	3	1	3	2
8	3	2	1	3
9	3	3	2	1

Examine columns 1 and 2—do the nine combinations of 1, 2, and 3 all appear in that column pair? Yes. Now examine columns 1 and 3—do the nine combinations of 1, 2, and 3 appear in that column pair? Yes, although in a different order. Examine columns 1 and 4—do the nine combinations appear in that column pair also? Yes they do. Continue on by examining other pairs of columns—2 and 3, 2 and 4, and finally 3 and 4. The $L_9(3^4)$ array is orthogonal; that is, choose any two columns, all the combinations will occur in all of the column pairs.

■■■■■■■■■■■■■■■■■■
Tool

The rdExpert tool from Phadke Associates implements the orthogonal array approach. See http://www. phadkeassociates. com

Note that not all combinations of 1s, 2s, and 3s appear in the array. For example, {1,1,2}, {1,2,1}, and {2,2,2) do not appear. Orthogonal arrays only guarantee that all the pair combinations exist in the array. Combinations such as {2,2,2} are triples, not pairs.

The following is an $L_{18}(3^5)$ orthogonal array. It has five columns, each containing a 1, 2, or 3. Examine columns 1 and 2 for the pair {1,1}. Does that pair exist in those two columns? Wait! Don't look at the array. From the definition of an orthogonal array, what is the answer? Yes, that pair exists along with every other pair of 1, 2, and 3. The pair {1,1} is in row 1. Note that {1,1} also appears in row 6. Returning to the original description of orthogonal arrays,

> An orthogonal array is a two-dimensional array of numbers that has this interesting property—choose any two columns in the array. All the pairwise combinations of its values will occur in every column pair.

This definition is not totally complete. Not only will all the pair combinations occur in the array, but if any pair occurs multiple times, all pairs will occur that same number of times. This is because orthogonal arrays are "balanced." Examine columns 3 and 5—look for {3,2}. That combination appears in rows 6 and 17.

	1	2	3	4	5
1	1	1	1	1	1
2	1	2	3	3	1
3	1	3	2	3	2
4	1	2	2	1	3
5	1	3	1	2	3
6	1	1	3	2	2
7	2	2	2	2	2
8	2	3	1	1	2
9	2	1	3	1	3
10	2	3	3	2	1
11	2	1	2	3	1
12	2	2	1	3	3
13	3	3	3	3	3
14	3	1	2	2	3
15	3	2	1	2	1
16	3	1	1	3	2
17	3	2	3	1	2
18	3	3	2	1	1

■■■■■■■■■■■■■■■■■■

Table 6-3

$L_{18}(3^5)$ Orthogonal Array

_____

In orthogonal arrays not all of the columns must have the same range of values (1..2, 1..3, 1..5, etc.). Some orthogonal arrays are mixed. The following is an $L_{18}(2^1 3^7)$ orthogonal array. It has one column of 1s and 2s, and seven columns of 1s, 2s, and 3s.

	1	2	3	4	5	6	7	8
1	1	1	1	1	1	1	1	1
2	1	1	2	2	2	2	2	2
3	1	1	3	3	3	3	3	3
4	1	2	1	1	2	2	3	3
5	1	2	2	2	3	3	1	1
6	1	2	3	3	1	1	2	2
7	1	3	1	2	1	3	2	3
8	1	3	2	3	2	1	3	1
9	1	3	3	1	3	2	1	2
10	2	1	1	3	3	2	2	1
11	2	1	2	1	1	3	3	2
12	2	1	3	2	2	1	1	3
13	2	2	1	2	3	1	3	2
14	2	2	2	3	1	2	1	3
15	2	2	3	1	2	3	2	1
16	2	3	1	3	2	3	1	2
17	2	3	2	1	3	1	2	3
18	2	3	3	2	1	2	3	1

■■■■■■■■■■■■■■■■■

Table 6-4

$L_{18}(2^13^7)$ Orthogonal Array

_____

■■■■■■■■■■■■■■■■■

Reference

Neil J.A. Sloane maintains a very comprehensive catalog of orthogonal arrays at http://www. research.att.com/ ~njas/oadir/ index.html

_____

Using Orthogonal Arrays

The process of using orthogonal arrays to select pairwise subsets for testing is:

1. Identify the variables.
2. Determine the number of choices for each variable.
3. Locate an orthogonal array which has a column for each variable and values within the columns that correspond to the choices for each variable.
4. Map the test problem onto the orthogonal array.
5. Construct the test cases.

If this seems rather vague at this point it's time for an example.

Web-based systems such as Brown & Donaldson and the Stateless University Registration System must operate in a number of environments. Let's execute the process step-by-step using an orthogonal array to choose test cases. Consider the first example in the introduction describing the software combinations a Web site must operate with.

1. **Identify the variables.**

    The variables are Browser, Plug-in, Client operating system, Server, and Server operating system.

2. **Determine the number of choices for each variable.**

    Browser – Internet Explorer 5.0, 5.5, and 6.0, Netscape 6.0, 6.1, and 7.0, Mozilla 1.1, and Opera 7 (8 choices).

    Plug-in – None, RealPlayer, and MediaPlayer (3 choices).

    Client operating system – Windows 95, 98, ME, NT, 2000, and XP (6 choices).

    Server – IIS, Apache, and WebLogic (3 choices).

    Server operating system – Windows NT, 2000, and Linux (3 choices).

    Multiplying 8 x 3 x 6 x 3 x 3 we find there are 1,296 combinations. For "complete" test coverage, each of these combinations should be tested.

3. **Locate an orthogonal array that has a column for each variable and values within the columns that correspond to the choices of each variable.**

What size array is needed? First, it must have five columns, one for each variable in this example. The first column must support eight different levels (1 through 8). The second column must support three levels (1 through 3). The third requires six levels. The fourth and the fifth each require three levels. The perfect size orthogonal array would be $8^1 6^1 3^3$ (one column of 1 through 8, one column of 1 through 6, and three columns of 1 through 3). Unfortunately, one of this exact size does not exist. When this occurs, we simply pick the next larger array.

The following orthogonal array meets our requirements. It's an $L_{64}(8^2 4^3)$ array. Orthogonal arrays can be found in a number of books and on the Web. A favorite book is *Quality Engineering Using Robust Design* by Madhav S. Phadke. In addition, an excellent catalog is maintained on the Web by Neil J.A. Sloane of AT&T. See http://www.research.att.com/~njas/oadir/index.html.

The requirement of $8^1 6^1$ (one column of 1 through 8 and 1 column of 1 through 6) is met by 8^2 (two columns of 1 through 8). The requirement of 3^3 (three columns of 1 through 3) is met by 4^3 (three columns of 1 through 4).

The number of combinations of all the values of all the variables is 1,296 and thus 1,296 test cases should be created and run for complete coverage. Using this orthogonal array, all pairs of all the values of all the variables can be covered in only sixty-four tests, a 95 percent reduction in the number of test cases.

■■■■■■■■■■■■■■■■■■
Important Note

As a tester you do not have to create orthogonal arrays. All you must do is locate one of the proper size and then perform the mapping of the test problem onto the array.

	1	2	3	4	5
1	1	1	1	1	1
2	1	4	3	4	4
3	1	4	2	4	4
4	1	1	4	1	1
5	1	3	5	3	3
6	1	2	7	2	2
7	1	2	6	2	2
8	1	3	8	3	3
9	3	4	1	3	3
10	3	1	3	2	2
11	3	1	2	2	2
12	3	4	4	3	3
13	3	2	5	1	1
14	3	3	7	4	4
15	3	3	6	4	4
16	3	2	8	1	1
17	2	3	1	2	1
18	2	2	3	3	4
19	2	2	2	3	4
20	2	3	4	2	1
21	2	1	5	4	3
22	2	4	7	1	2
23	2	4	6	1	2
24	2	1	8	4	3
25	4	2	1	4	3
26	4	3	3	1	2
27	4	3	2	1	2
28	4	2	4	4	3
29	4	4	5	2	1
30	4	1	7	3	4
31	4	1	6	3	4
32	4	4	8	2	1
33	5	2	1	4	2
34	5	3	3	1	3
35	5	3	2	1	3
36	5	2	4	4	2
37	5	4	5	2	4
38	5	1	7	3	1
39	5	1	6	3	1
40	5	4	8	2	4
41	7	3	1	2	4
42	7	2	3	3	1
43	7	2	2	3	1
44	7	3	4	2	4
45	7	1	5	4	2
46	7	4	7	1	3
47	7	4	6	1	3

■■■■■■■■■■■■■■■■■

Table 6-5

L_{64} $(8^2 4^3)$
Orthogonal Array

48	7	1	8	4	2
49	6	4	1	3	2
50	6	1	3	2	3
51	6	1	2	2	3
52	6	4	4	3	2
53	6	2	5	1	4
54	6	3	7	4	1
55	6	3	6	4	1
56	6	2	8	1	4
57	8	1	1	1	4
58	8	4	3	4	1
59	8	4	2	4	1
60	8	1	4	1	4
61	8	3	5	3	2
62	8	2	7	2	3
63	8	2	6	2	3
64	8	3	8	3	2

4. Map the test problem onto the orthogonal array.

The Browser choices will be mapped onto column 1 of the orthogonal array. Cells containing a 1 will represent IE 5.0; cells with a 2 will represent IE5.5; cells with a 3 will represent IE 6.0; etc. The mapping is:

> 1 ↔ IE 5.0
> 2 ↔ IE 5.5
> 3 ↔ IE 6.0
> 4 ↔ Netscape 6.0
> 5 ↔ Netscape 6.1
> 6 ↔ Netscape 7.0
> 7 ↔ Mozilla 1.1
> 8 ↔ Opera 7

Partially filling in the first column gives:

	Browser	2	3	4	5
1	IE 5.0	1	1	1	1
2	1	4	3	4	4
3	1	4	2	4	4
4	1	1	4	1	1
5	1	3	5	3	3
6	1	2	7	2	2
7	1	2	6	2	2
8	1	3	8	3	3
9	IE 6.0	4	1	3	3
10	3	1	3	2	2
11	3	1	2	2	2
12	3	4	4	3	3
13	3	2	5	1	1
14	3	3	7	4	4
15	3	3	6	4	4
16	3	2	8	1	1
17	IE 5.5	3	1	2	1
18	2	2	3	3	4
19	2	2	2	3	4
20	2	3	4	2	1
21	2	1	5	4	3
22	2	4	7	1	2
23	2	4	6	1	2
24	2	1	8	4	3
25	Net 6.0	2	1	4	3
26	4	3	3	1	2
27	4	3	2	1	2
28	4	2	4	4	3
29	4	4	5	2	1
30	4	1	7	3	4
31	4	1	6	3	4
32	4	4	8	2	1
33	Net 6.1	2	1	4	2
34	5	3	3	1	3
35	5	3	2	1	3
36	5	2	4	4	2
37	5	4	5	2	4
38	5	1	7	3	1
39	5	1	6	3	1
40	5	4	8	2	4
41	Moz 1.1	3	1	2	4
42	7	2	3	3	1
43	7	2	2	3	1
44	7	3	4	2	4
45	7	1	5	4	2
46	7	4	7	1	3
47	7	4	6	1	3

■■■■■■■■■■■■■■■■■■

Table 6-6

L_{64} $(8^2 4^3)$ with a partial mapping of its first column.

48	7	1	8	4	2
49	Net 7.0	4	1	3	2
50	6	1	3	2	3
51	6	1	2	2	3
52	6	4	4	3	2
53	6	2	5	1	4
54	6	3	7	4	1
55	6	3	6	4	1
56	6	2	8	1	4
57	Opera 7	1	1	1	4
58	8	4	3	4	1
59	8	4	2	4	1
60	8	1	4	1	4
61	8	3	5	3	2
62	8	2	7	2	3
63	8	2	6	2	3
64	8	3	8	3	2

Is it clear what is happening? In column 1 (which we have chosen to represent the Browser) every cell containing a 1 is being replaced with "IE 5.0." Every cell containing a 2 is being replaced with "IE 5.5." Every cell containing an 8 is being replaced with "Opera 7," etc.

We'll continue by completing the mapping (replacement) of all the cells in column 1. Note that the mapping between the variable values and the 1s, 2s, and 3s is totally arbitrary. There is no logical connection between "1" and IE 5.0 or "7" and Mozilla 1.1. But, although the initial assignment is arbitrary, once chosen, the assignments and use must remain consistent within each column.

	Browser	2	3	4	5
1	IE 5.0	1	1	1	1
2	IE 5.0	4	3	4	4
3	IE 5.0	4	2	4	4
4	IE 5.0	1	4	1	1
5	IE 5.0	3	5	3	3
6	IE 5.0	2	7	2	2
7	IE 5.0	2	6	2	2
8	IE 5.0	3	8	3	3
9	IE 6.0	4	1	3	3
10	IE 6.0	1	3	2	2
11	IE 6.0	1	2	2	2
12	IE 6.0	4	4	3	3
13	IE 6.0	2	5	1	1
14	IE 6.0	3	7	4	4
15	IE 6.0	3	6	4	4
16	IE 6.0	2	8	1	1
17	IE 5.5	3	1	2	1
18	IE 5.5	2	3	3	4
19	IE 5.5	2	2	3	4
20	IE 5.5	3	4	2	1
21	IE 5.5	1	5	4	3
22	IE 5.5	4	7	1	2
23	IE 5.5	4	6	1	2
24	IE 5.5	1	8	4	3
25	Net 6.0	2	1	4	3
26	Net 6.0	3	3	1	2
27	Net 6.0	3	2	1	2
28	Net 6.0	2	4	4	3
29	Net 6.0	4	5	2	1
30	Net 6.0	1	7	3	4
31	Net 6.0	1	6	3	4
32	Net 6.0	4	8	2	1
33	Net 6.1	2	1	4	2
34	Net 6.1	3	3	1	3
35	Net 6.1	3	2	1	3
36	Net 6.1	2	4	4	2
37	Net 6.1	4	5	2	4
38	Net 6.1	1	7	3	1
39	Net 6.1	1	6	3	1
40	Net 6.1	4	8	2	4
41	Moz 1.1	3	1	2	4
42	Moz 1.1	2	3	3	1
43	Moz 1.1	2	2	3	1
44	Moz 1.1	3	4	2	4
45	Moz 1.1	1	5	4	2
46	Moz 1.1	4	7	1	3
47	Moz 1.1	4	6	1	3

■■■■■■■■■■■■■■■■■

Table 6-7

L_{64} $(8^2 4^3)$ with a full mapping of its first column.

48	Moz 1.1	1	8	4	2
49	Net 7.0	4	1	3	2
50	Net 7.0	1	3	2	3
51	Net 7.0	1	2	2	3
52	Net 7.0	4	4	3	2
53	Net 7.0	2	5	1	4
54	Net 7.0	3	7	4	1
55	Net 7.0	3	6	4	1
56	Net 7.0	2	8	1	4
57	Opera 7	1	1	1	4
58	Opera 7	4	3	4	1
59	Opera 7	4	2	4	1
60	Opera 7	1	4	1	4
61	Opera 7	3	5	3	2
62	Opera 7	2	7	2	3
63	Opera 7	2	6	2	3
64	Opera 7	3	8	3	2

Now that the first column has been mapped, let's proceed to the next one. The Plug-in choices will be mapped onto column 2 of the array. Cells containing a 1 will represent None (No plug-in); cells with a 2 will represent RealPlayer; cells with a 3 will represent MediaPlayer; cells with a 4 will not be mapped at the present time. The mapping is:

1 ↔ None
2 ↔ RealPlayer
3 ↔ MediaPlayer
4 ↔ Not used (at this time)

Filling in the second column gives:

	Browser	Plug-in	3	4	5
1	IE 5.0	None	1	1	1
2	IE 5.0	4	3	4	4
3	IE 5.0	4	2	4	4
4	IE 5.0	None	4	1	1
5	IE 5.0	MediaPlayer	5	3	3
6	IE 5.0	RealPlayer	7	2	2
7	IE 5.0	RealPlayer	6	2	2
8	IE 5.0	MediaPlayer	8	3	3
9	IE 6.0	4	1	3	3
10	IE 6.0	None	3	2	2
11	IE 6.0	None	2	2	2
12	IE 6.0	4	4	3	3
13	IE 6.0	RealPlayer	5	1	1
14	IE 6.0	MediaPlayer	7	4	4
15	IE 6.0	MediaPlayer	6	4	4
16	IE 6.0	RealPlayer	8	1	1
17	IE 5.5	MediaPlayer	1	2	1
18	IE 5.5	RealPlayer	3	3	4
19	IE 5.5	RealPlayer	2	3	4
20	IE 5.5	MediaPlayer	4	2	1
21	IE 5.5	None	5	4	3
22	IE 5.5	4	7	1	2
23	IE 5.5	4	6	1	2
24	IE 5.5	None	8	4	3
25	Net 6.0	RealPlayer	1	4	3
26	Net 6.0	MediaPlayer	3	1	2
27	Net 6.0	MediaPlayer	2	1	2
28	Net 6.0	RealPlayer	4	4	3
29	Net 6.0	4	5	2	1
30	Net 6.0	None	7	3	4
31	Net 6.0	None	6	3	4
32	Net 6.0	4	8	2	1
33	Net 6.1	RealPlayer	1	4	2
34	Net 6.1	MediaPlayer	3	1	3
35	Net 6.1	MediaPlayer	2	1	3
36	Net 6.1	RealPlayer	4	4	2
37	Net 6.1	4	5	2	4
38	Net 6.1	None	7	3	1
39	Net 6.1	None	6	3	1
40	Net 6.1	4	8	2	4
41	Moz 1.1	MediaPlayer	1	2	4
42	Moz 1.1	RealPlayer	3	3	1
43	Moz 1.1	RealPlayer	2	3	1
44	Moz 1.1	MediaPlayer	4	2	4
45	Moz 1.1	None	5	4	2
46	Moz 1.1	4	7	1	3

■■■■■■■■■■■■■■■■■■

Table 6-8

L_{64} $(8^2 4^3)$ with a full mapping of its first and second columns.

———————————

47	Moz 1.1	4	6	1	3
48	Moz 1.1	None	8	4	2
49	Net 7.0	4	1	3	2
50	Net 7.0	None	3	2	3
51	Net 7.0	None	2	2	3
52	Net 7.0	4	4	3	2
53	Net 7.0	RealPlayer	5	1	4
54	Net 7.0	MediaPlayer	7	4	1
55	Net 7.0	MediaPlayer	6	4	1
56	Net 7.0	RealPlayer	8	1	4
57	Opera 7	None	1	1	4
58	Opera 7	4	3	4	1
59	Opera 7	4	2	4	1
60	Opera 7	None	4	1	4
61	Opera 7	MediaPlayer	5	3	2
62	Opera 7	RealPlayer	7	2	3
63	Opera 7	RealPlayer	6	2	3
64	Opera 7	MediaPlayer	8	3	2

Now that the first and second columns have been mapped, let's proceed to map the next three columns simultaneously.

The mapping for Client operating system is:

> 1 ↔ Windows 95
> 2 ↔ Windows 98
> 3 ↔ Windows ME
> 4 ↔ Windows NT
> 5 ↔ Windows 2000
> 6 ↔ Windows XP
> 7 ↔ Not used (at this time)
> 8 ↔ Not used (at this time)

The mapping for Servers is:

> 1 ↔ IIS
> 2 ↔ Apache
> 3 ↔ WebLogic
> 4 ↔ Not used (at this time)

The mapping for Server operating system is:

$1 \leftrightarrow$ Windows NT

$2 \leftrightarrow$ Windows 2000

$3 \leftrightarrow$ Linux

$4 \leftrightarrow$ Not used (at this time)

Filling in the remainder of the columns gives:

	Browser	Plug-in	Client OS	Server	Server OS
1	IE 5.0	None	Win 95	IIS	Win NT
2	IE 5.0	4	Win ME	4	4
3	IE 5.0	4	Win 98	4	4
4	IE 5.0	None	Win NT	IIS	Win NT
5	IE 5.0	MediaPlayer	Win 2000	WebLogic	Linux
6	IE 5.0	RealPlayer	7	Apache	Win 2000
7	IE 5.0	RealPlayer	Win XP	Apache	Win 2000
8	IE 5.0	MediaPlayer	8	WebLogic	Linux
9	IE 6.0	4	Win 95	WebLogic	Linux
10	IE 6.0	None	Win ME	Apache	Win 2000
11	IE 6.0	None	Win 98	Apache	Win 2000
12	IE 6.0	4	Win NT	WebLogic	Linux
13	IE 6.0	RealPlayer	Win 2000	IIS	Win NT
14	IE 6.0	MediaPlayer	7	4	4
15	IE 6.0	MediaPlayer	Win XP	4	4
16	IE 6.0	RealPlayer	8	IIS	Win NT
17	IE 5.5	MediaPlayer	Win 95	Apache	Win NT
18	IE 5.5	RealPlayer	Win ME	WebLogic	4
19	IE 5.5	RealPlayer	Win 98	WebLogic	4
20	IE 5.5	MediaPlayer	Win NT	Apache	Win NT
21	IE 5.5	None	Win 2000	4	Linux
22	IE 5.5	4	7	IIS	Win 2000
23	IE 5.5	4	Win XP	IIS	Win 2000
24	IE 5.5	None	8	4	Linux
25	Net 6.0	RealPlayer	Win 95	4	Linux
26	Net 6.0	MediaPlayer	Win ME	IIS	Win 2000
27	Net 6.0	MediaPlayer	Win 98	IIS	Win 2000
28	Net 6.0	RealPlayer	Win NT	4	Linux
29	Net 6.0	4	Win 2000	Apache	Win NT
30	Net 6.0	None	7	WebLogic	4
31	Net 6.0	None	Win XP	WebLogic	4
32	Net 6.0	4	8	Apache	Win NT
33	Net 6.1	RealPlayer	Win 95	4	Win 2000
34	Net 6.1	MediaPlayer	Win ME	IIS	Linux
35	Net 6.1	MediaPlayer	Win 98	IIS	Linux

■■■■■■■■■■■■■■■■■

Table 6-9

L_{64} $(8^2 4^3)$ with a full mapping of all its columns.

36	Net 6.1	RealPlayer	Win NT	4	Win 2000
37	Net 6.1	4	Win 2000	Apache	4
38	Net 6.1	None	7	WebLogic	Win NT
39	Net 6.1	None	Win XP	WebLogic	1 Win NT
40	Net 6.1	4	8	Apache	4
41	Moz 1.1	MediaPlayer	Win 95	Apache	4
42	Moz 1.1	RealPlayer	Win ME	WebLogic	Win NT
43	Moz 1.1	RealPlayer	Win 98	WebLogic	Win NT
44	Moz 1.1	MediaPlayer	Win NT	Apache	4
45	Moz 1.1	None	Win 2000	4	Win 2000
46	Moz 1.1	4	7	IIS	Linux
47	Moz 1.1	4	Win XP	IIS	Linux
48	Moz 1.1	None	8	4	Win 2000
49	Net 7.0	4	Win 95	WebLogic	Win 2000
50	Net 7.0	None	Win ME	Apache	Linux
51	Net 7.0	None	Win 98	Apache	Linux
52	Net 7.0	4	Win NT	WebLogic	Win 2000
53	Net 7.0	RealPlayer	Win 2000	IIS	4
54	Net 7.0	MediaPlayer	7	4	Win NT
55	Net 7.0	MediaPlayer	Win XP	4	Win NT
56	Net 7.0	RealPlayer	8	IIS	4
57	Opera 7	None	Win 95	IIS	4
58	Opera 7	4	Win ME	4	Win NT
59	Opera 7	4	Win 98	4	Win NT
60	Opera 7	None	Win NT	IIS	4
61	Opera 7	MediaPlayer	Win 2000	WebLogic	Win 2000
62	Opera 7	RealPlayer	7	Apache	Linux
63	Opera 7	RealPlayer	Win XP	Apache	Linux
64	Opera 7	MediaPlayer	8	WebLogic	Win 2000

Were it not for the few cells that remain unassigned, the mapping of the orthogonal array, and thus the selection of the test cases, would be completed. What about the unassigned cells—first, why do they exist?; second, what should be done with them?

The unassigned cells exist because the orthogonal array chosen was "too big." The perfect size would be an $8^1 6^1 3^3$ array; that is, one column that varies from 1 to 8; one column that varies from 1 to 6; and three columns that vary from 1 to 3. Unfortunately, that specific size orthogonal array does not exist. Orthogonal arrays cannot be constructed for any arbitrary size parameters. They come in fixed, "quantum" sizes. You can construct one "this big"; you can construct one "that big"; but you cannot necessarily construct one in-between. Famous Software Tester Mick Jagger gives excellent advice regarding this, "You can't always get what you want, But if you try sometimes, You just might find, you get what you need."

If the perfect size array does not exist, choose one that is slightly bigger and apply these two rules to deal with the "excess." The first rule deals with extra columns. If the orthogonal array chosen has more columns than needed for a particular test scenario, simply delete them. The array will remain orthogonal. The second rule deals with extra values for a variable. In the current example, column 3 runs from 1 to 8 but only 1 through 6 is needed. It is tempting to delete the rows that contain these cells but DON'T. The "orthogonalness" may be lost. Each row in the array exists to provide at least one pair combination that appears nowhere else in the array. If you delete a row, you lose that test case. Instead of deleting them, simply convert the extra cells to valid values. Some automated tools randomly choose from the set of valid values for each cell while others choose one valid value and use it in every cell within a column. Either approach is acceptable. Using this second approach, we'll complete the orthogonal array. Note that it may be difficult to maintain the "balanced" aspect of the array when assigning values to these extra cells.

Famous Software Tester

Mick Jagger

	Browser	Plug-in	Client OS	Server	Server OS
1	IE 5.0	None	Win 95	IIS	Win NT
2	IE 5.0	None	Win ME	IIS	Win NT
3	IE 5.0	None	Win 98	IIS	Win NT
4	IE 5.0	None	Win NT	IIS	Win NT
5	IE 5.0	MediaPlayer	Win 2000	WebLogic	Linux
6	IE 5.0	RealPlayer	Win 95	Apache	Win 2000
7	IE 5.0	RealPlayer	Win XP	Apache	Win 2000
8	IE 5.0	MediaPlayer	Win 98	WebLogic	Linux
9	IE 6.0	None	Win 95	WebLogic	Linux
10	IE 6.0	None	Win ME	Apache	Win 2000
11	IE 6.0	None	Win 98	Apache	Win 2000
12	IE 6.0	None	Win NT	WebLogic	Linux
13	IE 6.0	RealPlayer	Win 2000	IIS	Win NT
14	IE 6.0	MediaPlayer	Win 95	IIS	Win NT
15	IE 6.0	MediaPlayer	Win XP	IIS	Win NT
16	IE 6.0	RealPlayer	Win 98	IIS	Win NT
17	IE 5.5	MediaPlayer	Win 95	Apache	Win NT
18	IE 5.5	RealPlayer	Win ME	WebLogic	Win NT
19	IE 5.5	RealPlayer	Win 98	WebLogic	Win NT
20	IE 5.5	MediaPlayer	Win NT	Apache	Win NT
21	IE 5.5	None	Win 2000	IIS	Linux
22	IE 5.5	None	Win 95	IIS	Win 2000
23	IE 5.5	None	Win XP	IIS	Win 2000
24	IE 5.5	None	Win 98	IIS	Linux
25	Net 6.0	RealPlayer	Win 95	IIS	Linux
26	Net 6.0	MediaPlayer	Win ME	IIS	Win 2000
27	Net 6.0	MediaPlayer	Win 98	IIS	Win 2000
28	Net 6.0	RealPlayer	Win NT	IIS	Linux
29	Net 6.0	None	Win 2000	Apache	Win NT
30	Net 6.0	None	Win 95	WebLogic	Win NT
31	Net 6.0	None	Win XP	WebLogic	Win NT
32	Net 6.0	None	Win 98	Apache	Win NT
33	Net 6.1	RealPlayer	Win 95	IIS	Win 2000
34	Net 6.1	MediaPlayer	Win ME	IIS	Linux
35	Net 6.1	MediaPlayer	Win 98	IIS	Linux
36	Net 6.1	RealPlayer	Win NT	IIS	Win 2000
37	Net 6.1	None	Win 2000	Apache	Win NT
38	Net 6.1	None	Win 95	WebLogic	Win NT
39	Net 6.1	None	Win XP	WebLogic	Win NT
40	Net 6.1	None	Win 98	Apache	Win NT
41	Moz 1.1	MediaPlayer	Win 95	Apache	Win NT
42	Moz 1.1	RealPlayer	Win ME	WebLogic	Win NT
43	Moz 1.1	RealPlayer	Win 98	WebLogic	Win NT
44	Moz 1.1	MediaPlayer	Win NT	Apache	Win NT
45	Moz 1.1	None	Win 2000	IIS	Win 2000
46	Moz 1.1	None	Win 95	IIS	Linux
47	Moz 1.1	None	Win XP	IIS	Linux

■■■■■■■■■■■■■■■■■■

Table 6-10

L_{64} ($8^2 4^3$) with a full mapping of all its columns including the "extra" cells.

48	Moz 1.1	None	Win 98	IIS	Win 2000
49	Net 7.0	None	Win 95	WebLogic	Win 2000
50	Net 7.0	None	Win ME	Apache	Linux
51	Net 7.0	None	Win 98	Apache	Linux
52	Net 7.0	None	Win NT	WebLogic	Win 2000
53	Net 7.0	RealPlayer	Win 2000	IIS	Win NT
54	Net 7.0	MediaPlayer	Win 95	IIS	Win NT
55	Net 7.0	MediaPlayer	Win XP	IIS	Win NT
56	Net 7.0	RealPlayer	Win 98	IIS	Win NT
57	Opera 7	None	Win 95	IIS	Win NT
58	Opera 7	None	Win ME	IIS	Win NT
59	Opera 7	None	Win 98	IIS	Win NT
60	Opera 7	None	Win NT	IIS	Win NT
61	Opera 7	MediaPlayer	Win 2000	WebLogic	Win 2000
62	Opera 7	RealPlayer	Win 95	Apache	Linux
63	Opera 7	RealPlayer	Win XP	Apache	Linux
64	Opera 7	MediaPlayer	Win 98	WebLogic	Win 2000

5. Construct the test cases.

Now, all that remains is to construct a test case for each row in the orthogonal array. Note that the array specifies only the input conditions. An oracle (usually the tester) is required to determine the expected result for each test.

Allpairs Algorithm

Using orthogonal arrays is one way to identify all the pairs. A second way is to use an algorithm that generates the pairs directly without resorting to an "external" device like an orthogonal array.

James Bach presents an algorithm to generate all pairs in *Lessons Learned in Software Testing*. In addition, he provides a program called "Allpairs" that will generate the all pairs combinations. It is available at http://www.satisfice.com. Click on "Test Methodology" and look for Allpairs. Let's apply the Allpairs algorithm to the previous Web site testing problem.

■■■■■■■■■■■■■■■■■
Reference

James Bach provides a tool to generate all pairs combinations at http://www.satisfice.com. Click on Test Methodology and look for Allpairs.

Ward Cunningham provides further discussion and the source code for a Java program to generate all pairs combinations at http://fit.c2.com/wiki.cgi?AllPairs.

After downloading and unzipping, to use Allpairs create a tab-delimited table of the variables and their values. If you are a Windows user, the easiest way is to launch Excel, enter the data into the spreadsheet, and then SaveAs a .txt file. The following table was created and saved as input.txt.

Browser	Client OS	Plug-in	Server	Server OS
IE 5.0	Win 95	None	IIS	Win NT
IE 5.5	Win 98	Real Player	Apache	Win 2000
IE 6.0	Win ME	Media Player	WebLogic	Linux
Netscape 6.0	Win NT			
Netscape 6.1	Win 2000			
Netscape 7.0	Win XP			
Mozilla 1.1				
Opera 7				

■■■■■■■■■■■■■■■■■

Table 6-11

Input to the Allpairs program.

Then run the Allpairs program by typing:

allpairs input.txt > output.txt

where output.txt will contain the list of all pairs test cases. The following table was created:

	Browser	Client OS	Plug-in	Server	Server OS
1	IE 5.0	Win 95	None	IIS	Win NT
2	IE 5.0	Win 98	Real Player	Apache	Win 2000
3	IE 5.0	Win ME	Media Player	WebLogic	Linux
4	IE 5.5	Win 95	Real Player	WebLogic	Win NT
5	IE 5.5	Win 98	None	IIS	Linux
6	IE 5.5	Win ME	None	Apache	Win 2000
7	IE 6.0	Win 95	Media Player	Apache	Linux
8	IE 6.0	Win 98	Real Player	IIS	Win NT
9	IE 6.0	Win ME	None	WebLogic	Win 2000
10	Netscape 6.0	Win ME	Real Player	IIS	Linux
11	Netscape 6.0	Win NT	Media Player	IIS	Win 2000
12	Netscape 6.0	Win 2000	None	Apache	Win NT
13	Netscape 6.1	Win NT	None	WebLogic	Linux
14	Netscape 6.1	Win 2000	Media Player	IIS	Win 2000
15	Netscape 6.1	Win XP	Real Player	Apache	Win NT
16	Netscape 7.0	Win NT	Real Player	Apache	Win NT
17	Netscape 7.0	Win 2000	Media Player	WebLogic	Linux
18	Netscape 7.0	Win XP	Media Player	IIS	Win 2000
19	Mozilla 1.1	Win XP	Media Player	WebLogic	Win NT

■■■■■■■■■■■■■■■■■

Table 6-12

Output from the Allpairs program.

20	Mozilla 1.1	Win 98	Media Player	Apache	Linux
21	Mozilla 1.1	Win 95	Real Player	IIS	Win 2000
22	Opera 7	Win XP	None	WebLogic	Linux
23	Opera 7	Win 98	Real Player	WebLogic	Win 2000
24	Opera 7	Win ME	Media Player	Apache	Win NT
25	IE 5.5	Win 2000	Real Player	~WebLogic	~Linux
26	IE 5.5	Win NT	Media Player	~IIS	~Win NT
27	Netscape 6.0	Win 95	~None	WebLogic	~Win 2000
28	Netscape 7.0	Win 95	None	~Apache	~Linux
29	Mozilla 1.1	Win ME	None	~IIS	~Win NT
30	Opera 7	Win NT	~Real Player	IIS	~Linux
31	IE 5.0	Win NT	~None	~Apache	~Win 2000
32	IE 5.0	Win 2000	~Real Player	~IIS	~Win NT
33	IE 5.0	Win XP	~None	~WebLogic	~Linux
34	IE 5.5	Win XP	~Real Player	~Apache	~Win 2000
35	IE 6.0	Win 2000	~None	~Apache	~Win 2000
36	IE 6.0	Win NT	~Real Player	~WebLogic	~Win NT
37	IE 6.0	Win XP	~Media Player	~IIS	~Linux
38	Netscape 6.0	Win 98	~Media Player	~WebLogic	~Win NT
39	Netscape 6.0	Win XP	~Real Player	~Apache	~Linux
40	Netscape 6.1	Win 95	~Media Player	~Apache	~Win 2000
41	Netscape 6.1	Win 98	~None	~IIS	~Win NT
42	Netscape 6.1	Win ME	~Real Player	~WebLogic	~Linux
43	Netscape 7.0	Win 98	~None	~WebLogic	~Win 2000
44	Netscape 7.0	Win ME	~Real Player	~IIS	~Win NT
45	Mozilla 1.1	Win NT	~None	~Apache	~Linux
46	Mozilla 1.1	Win 2000	~Real Player	~WebLogic	~Win 2000
47	Opera 7	Win 95	~Media Player	~IIS	~Win NT
48	Opera 7	Win 2000	~None	~Apache	~Win 2000

When a particular value in the test case doesn't matter, because all of its pairings have already been selected, it is marked with a ~. Bach's algorithm chooses the value that has been paired the fewest times relative to the others in the test case. Any other value could be substituted for one prefixed with a ~ and all pairs coverage would still be maintained. This might be done to test more commonly used or more critical combinations more often. In addition, Bach's program displays information on how the pairings were done. It lists each pair, shows how many times that pair occurs in the table, and indicates each test case that contains that pair.

Because of the "balanced" nature of orthogonal arrays, that approach required sixty-four test cases. The "unbalanced" nature of the all pairs selection algorithm requires only forty-eight test cases, a savings of 25 percent.

Note that the combinations chosen by the Orthogonal Array method may not be the same as those chosen by Allpairs. It does not matter. What does matter is that all of the pair combinations of parameters are chosen. Those are the combinations we want to test.

Proponents of the Allpairs algorithm point out that given a problem with 100 parameters, each capable of taking on one of two values, 101 test cases would be required using a (balanced) orthogonal array while the un-balanced all pairs approach requires only ten tests. Since many applications have large numbers of inputs that take on only a few values each, they argue the all pairs approach is superior.

■■■■■■■■■■■■■■■■■■
Tool

The AETG tool from Telcordia implements the all-pairs testing approach. See http://aetgweb. argreenhouse.com.

Final Comments

In some situations, constraints exist between certain choices of some of the variables. For example, Microsoft's IIS and Apple's MacOS are not compatible. It is certain that the pairwise techniques will choose that combination for test. (Remember, it does select **all** the pairs.) When creating pairwise subsets by hand, honoring these various constraints can be difficult. Both the rdExpert and AETG tools have this ability. You define the constraints and the tool selects pairs meeting those constraints.

Given the two approaches to pairwise testing, orthogonal arrays and the Allpairs algorithm, which is more effective? One expert, who favors orthogonal arrays, believes that the coverage provided by Allpairs is substantially inferior. He notes that the uniform distribution of test points in the domain offers some coverage against faults that are more complex than double-mode faults. Another expert, who favors the Allpairs approach, notes that Allpairs does, in fact, test all the pairs, which is the goal. He claims there is no evidence that the orthogonal array approach detects more defects. He also notes that the Allpairs tool is available free on the Web. What both experts acknowledge is that no documented studies exist comparing the efficacy of one approach over the other.

The exciting hope of pairwise testing is that by creating and running between 1 percent to 20 percent of the tests you will find between 70 percent and 85 percent of the total defects. There is no promise here, only a hope. Many others have experienced this significant result. Try this technique. Discover whether it works for you.

Cohen reported that in addition to reducing the number of test cases and increasing the defect find rate, test cases created by the Allpairs algorithm also provided better code coverage. A set of 300 randomly selected tests achieved 67 percent statement coverage and 58 percent decision coverage while the 200 all pairs test cases achieved 92 percent block coverage and 85 percent decision coverage, a significant increase in coverage with fewer test cases.

One final comment—it is possible that certain important combinations may be missed by both pairwise approaches. The 80:20 rule tells us that combinations are not uniformly important. Use your judgment to determine if certain additional tests should be created for those combinations.

In the previous example we can be assured that the distribution of browsers is not identical. It would be truly amazing if 12.5 percent of our users had IE 5.0, 12.5 percent had IE 5.5, 12.5 percent had IE 6.0, etc. Certain combinations occur more frequently than others. In addition, some combinations exist that, while used infrequently, absolutely positively must work properly—"shut down the nuclear reactor" is a good example. In case pairwise misses an important combination, please add that combination to your test cases.

Applicability and Limitations

Like other test design approaches previously presented, pairwise testing can significantly reduce the number of test cases that must be created and executed. It is equally applicable at the unit, integration, system, and acceptance test levels. All it requires are combinations of inputs, each taking on various values, that result in a combinatorial explosion, too many combinations to test.

Remember, there is no underlying "software defect physics" that guarantees pairwise testing will be of benefit. There is only one way to know—try it.

Summary

- When the number of combinations to test is very large, do not to attempt to test all combinations for all the values for all the variables, but test **all pairs** of variables. This significantly reduces the number of tests that must be created and run.

- Studies suggest that most defects are either single-mode defects (the function under test simply does not work) or double-mode defects (the pairing of this function/module with that function/module fails). Pairwise testing defines a minimal subset that guides us to test for all single-mode and double-mode defects. The success of this technique on many projects, both documented and undocumented, is a great motivation for its use.

- An orthogonal array is a two-dimensional array of numbers that has this interesting property—choose any two columns in the array, all the combinations will occur in every column pair.

- There is no underlying "software defect physics" that guarantees pairwise testing will be of benefit. There is only one way to know—try it.

Practice

1. Neither the Brown & Donaldson nor the Stateless University Registration System case studies contain huge numbers of combinations suitable for the pairwise testing approach. As exercises, use the orthogonal array and/or all pairs technique on the other two examples in this chapter. Determine the set of pairwise test cases using the chosen technique.

   a. A bank has created a new data processing system that is ready for testing. This bank has different kinds of customers—consumers, very important consumers, businesses, and non-profits; different kinds of accounts—checking, savings, mortgages, consumer loans, and commercial loans; they operate in different states, each with different regulations—California, Nevada, Utah, Idaho, Arizona, and New Mexico.

   b. In an object-oriented system, an object of class A can send a message containing a parameter P to an object of class X. Classes B, C, and D inherit from A so they too can send the message. Classes Q, R, S, and T inherit from P so they too can be passed as the parameter. Classes Y and Z inherit from X so they too can receive the message.

References

Brownlie, Robert, et al. "Robust Testing of AT&T PMX/StarMAIL Using OATS," *AT&T Technical Journal*, Vol. 71, No. 3, May/June 1992, pp. 41–47.

Cohen, D.M., et al. "The AETG System: An Approach to Testing Based on Combinatorial Design." *IEEE Transactions on Software Engineering*, Vol. 23, No. 7, July, 1997.

Kaner, Cem, James Bach, and Bret Pettichord (2002). *Lessons Learned in Software Testing: A Context-Driven Approach*. John Wiley & Sons.

Kuhn, D. Richard and Michael J. Reilly. "An Investigation of the Applicability of Design of Experiments to Software Testing," 27th NASA/IEEE Software Engineering Workshop, NASA Goddard Space Flight Center, 4-6 December, 2002. http://csrc.nist.gov/staff/kuhn/kuhn-reilly-02.pdf

Mandl, Robert. "Orthogonal Latin Squares: An Application of Experiment Design to Compiler Testing," *Communications of the ACM,* Vol. 128, No. 10, October 1985, pp. 1054–1058.

Phadke, Madhav S. (1989). *Quality Engineering Using Robust Design*. Prentice-Hall.

Wallace, Delores R. and D. Richard Kuhn. "Failure Modes In Medical Device Software: An Analysis Of 15 Years Of Recall Data," *International Journal of Reliability, Quality, and Safety Engineering*, Vol. 8, No. 4, 2001.

Chapter 7 –
State-Transition Testing

*Colonel Cleatus Yorbville had been one seriously bored
astronaut for the first few months of his diplomatic mission on
the third planet of the Frangelicus XIV system, but all that had
changed on the day he'd discovered that his tiny, multipedal and
infinitely hospitable alien hosts were not only edible but tasted
remarkably like that stuff that's left on the pan after you've made
cinnamon buns and burned them a little.*

— Mark Silcox

Introduction

S tate-Transition diagrams, like decision tables, are another excellent tool to capture certain types of system requirements and to document internal system design. These diagrams document the events that come into and are processed by a system as well as the system's responses. Unlike decision tables, they specify very little in terms of processing rules. When a system must remember something about what has happened before or when valid and invalid orders of operations exist, state-transition diagrams are excellent tools to record this information.

These diagrams are also vital tools in the tester's personal toolbox. Unfortunately, many analysts, designers, programmers, and testers are not familiar with this technique.

Technique

State-Transition Diagrams

It is easier to introduce state-transition diagrams by example rather than by formal definition. Since neither Brown & Donaldson nor the Stateless University Registration System has substantial state-transition based requirements let's consider a different example. To get to Stateless U, we need an airline reservation. Let's call our favorite carrier (Grace L. Ferguson Airline & Storm Door Company) to make a reservation. We provide some information including departure and destination cities, dates, and times. A reservation agent, acting as our interface to the airline's reservation system, uses that information to make a reservation. At that point, the **Reservation** is in the **Made** state. In addition, the system creates and starts a timer. Each reservation has certain rules about when the reservation must be paid for. These rules are based on destination, class of service, dates, etc. If this timer expires before the reservation is paid for, the reservation is cancelled by the system. In state-transition notation this information is recorded as:

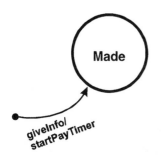

The circle represents one state of the **Reservation**—in this case the **Made** state. The arrow shows the transition into the **Made** state. The description on the arrow, **giveInfo**, is an event that comes into the system from the outside world. The command after the "**/**" denotes an action of the system; in this case **startPayTimer**. The black dot indicates the starting point of the diagram.

Sometime after the **Reservation** is made, but (hopefully) before the **PayTimer** expires, the **Reservation** is paid for. This is represented by the arrow labeled **PayMoney**. When the **Reservation** is paid it transitions from the **Made** state to the **Paid** state.

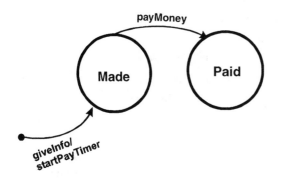

Before we proceed let's define the terms more formally:

- State (represented by a circle)—A state is a condition in which a system is waiting for one or more events. States "remember" inputs the system has received in the past and define how the system should respond to subsequent events when they occur. These events may cause state-transitions and/or initiate actions. The state is generally represented by the values of one or more variables within a system.

- Transition (represented by an arrow)—A transition represents a change from one state to another caused by an event.

- Event (represented by a label on a transition)—An event is something that causes the system to change state. Generally, it is an event in the outside world that enters the system through its interface. Sometimes it is generated within the system such as **Timer expires** or **Quantity on Hand goes below Reorder Point**. Events are considered to be instantaneous. Events can be independent or causally related (event B cannot take place before event A). When an event occurs, the system can change state or remain in the same state and/or execute an action. Events may have parameters associated with them. For example, **Pay Money** may indicate **Cash, Check, Debit Card**, or **Credit Card**.

- Action (represented by a command following a "/")—An action is an operation initiated because of a state change. It could be **print a Ticket, display a Screen, turn on a Motor**, etc. Often these actions cause something to be created that are outputs of the system. Note that actions occur on transitions between states. The states themselves are passive.

- The entry point on the diagram is shown by a black dot while the exit point is shown by a bulls-eye symbol.

This notation was created by Mealy. An alternate notation has been defined by Moore but is less frequently used. For a much more in-depth discussion of state-transition diagrams see Fowler and Scott's book, *UML Distilled: A Brief Guide To The Standard Object Modeling Language*. It discusses more complex issues such as partitioned and nested state-transition diagrams.

Note that the state-transition diagram represents one specific entity (in this case a **Reservation**). It describes the states of a reservation, the events that affect the reservation, the transitions of the reservation from one state to another, and actions that are initiated by the reservation. A common mistake is to mix different entities into one state-transition diagram. An example might be mixing **Reservation** and **Passenger** with events and actions corresponding to each.

From the **Paid** state the **Reservation** transitions to the **Ticketed** state when the **print** command (an event) is issued. Note that in addition to entering the **Ticketed** state, a **Ticket** is output by the system.

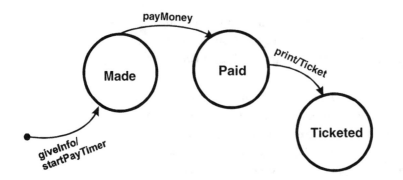

■■■■■■■■■■■■■■■■■■
Figure 7-3

The Reservation
transitions to the
Ticketed state.
─────────

From the **Ticketed** state we **giveTicket** to the gate agent to board
the plane.

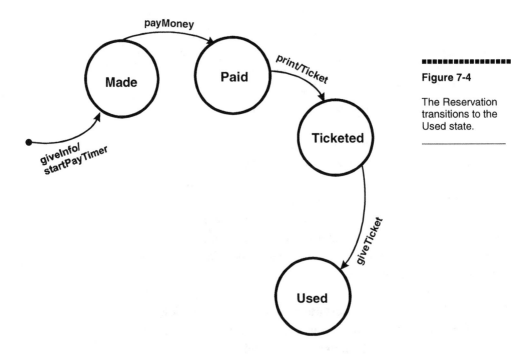

■■■■■■■■■■■■■■■■■■
Figure 7-4

The Reservation
transitions to the
Used state.
─────────

After some other action or period of time, not indicated on this diagram, the state-transition path ends at the bulls-eye symbol.

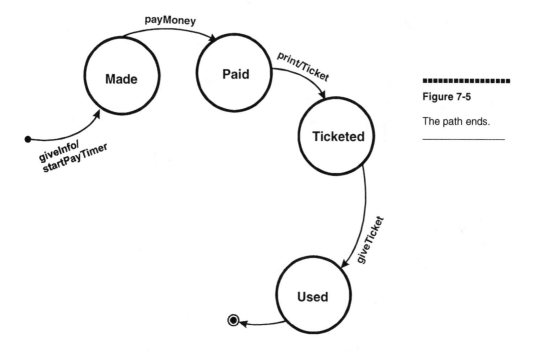

Figure 7-5

The path ends.

Does this diagram show all the possible states, events, and transitions in the life of a **Reservation**? No. If the **Reservation** is not paid for in the time allotted (the **PayTimer** expires), it is cancelled for non-payment.

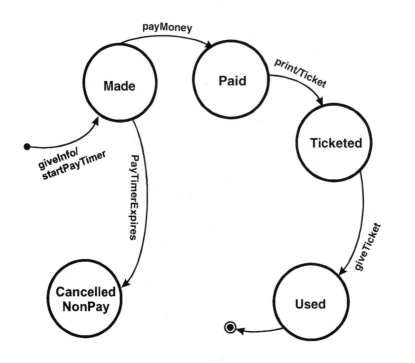

Figure 7-6

The PayTimer expires and the Reservation is cancelled for non-payment.

Finished yet? No. Customers sometimes cancel their reservations. From the **Made** state the customer (through the reservation agent) asks to **cancel** the **Reservation**. A new state, **Cancelled By Customer,** is required.

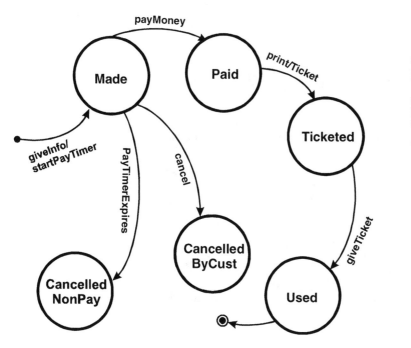

Figure 7-7

Cancel the
Reservation from
the Made state.

In addition, a **Reservation** can be cancelled from the **Paid** state.
In this case a **Refund** should be generated and leave the system.
The resulting state again is **Cancelled By Customer**.

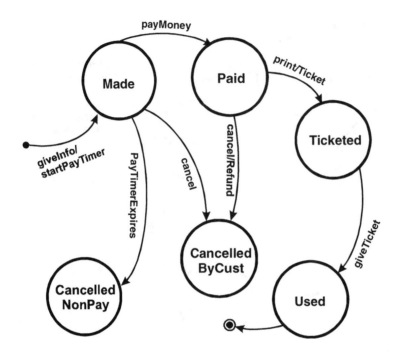

Figure 7-8

Cancellation from
the Paid state.

One final addition. From the **Ticketed** state the customer can
cancel the **Reservation**. In that case a **Refund** should be
generated and the next state should be **Cancelled by Customer**.
But this is not sufficient. The airline will generate a refund but
only when it receives the printed **Ticket** from the customer. This
introduces one new notational element—square brackets [] that
contain a conditional that can be evaluated either **True** or **False**.
This conditional acts as a guard allowing the transition only if
the condition is true.

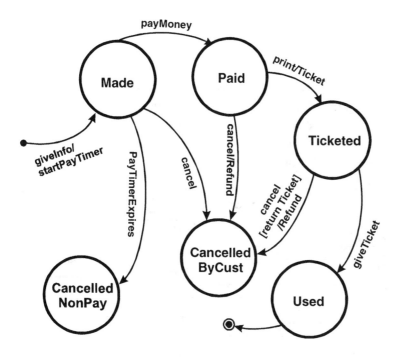

Figure 7-9

Cancellation from
the Ticketed state.

Note that the diagram is still incomplete. No arrows and bulls-eyes emerge from the **Cancelled** states. Perhaps we could reinstate a reservation from the **Cancelled NonPay** state. We could continue expanding the diagram to include seat selection, flight cancellation, and other significant events affecting the reservation but this is sufficient to illustrate the technique.

As described, state-transition diagrams express complex system rules and interactions in a very compact notation. Hopefully, when this complexity exists, analysts and designers will have created state-transition diagrams to document system requirements and to guide their design.

State-Transition Tables

A state-transition diagram is not the only way to document system behavior. The diagrams may be easier to comprehend, but state-transition tables may be easier to use in a complete and systematic manner. State-transition tables consist of four columns—Current State, Event, Action, and Next State.

Current State	Event	Action	Next State
null	giveInfo	startPayTimer	Made
null	payMoney	--	null
null	print	--	null
null	giveTicket	--	null
null	cancel	--	null
null	PayTimerExpires	--	null
Made	giveInfo	--	Made
Made	payMoney	--	Paid
Made	print	--	Made
Made	giveTicket	--	Made
Made	cancel	--	Can-Cust
Made	PayTimerExpires	--	Can-NonPay
Paid	giveInfo	--	Paid
Paid	payMoney	--	Paid
Paid	print	Ticket	Ticketed
Paid	giveTicket	--	Paid
Paid	cancel	Refund	Can-Cust
Paid	PayTimerExpires	--	Paid
Ticketed	giveInfo	--	Ticketed
Ticketed	payMoney	--	Ticketed
Ticketed	print	--	Ticketed
Ticketed	giveTicket	--	Used
Ticketed	cancel	Refund	Can-Cust
Ticketed	PayTimerExpires	--	Ticketed
Used	giveInfo	--	Used
Used	payMoney	--	Used
Used	print	--	Used
Used	giveTicket	--	Used
Used	cancel	--	Used
Used	PayTimerExpires	--	Used
Can-NonPay	giveInfo	--	Can-NonPay

▪▪▪▪▪▪▪▪▪▪▪▪▪▪▪▪▪▪

Table 7-1

State-Transition table for Reservation.

Can-NonPay	payMoney	--	Can-NonPay
Can-NonPay	print	--	Can-NonPay
Can-NonPay	giveTicket	--	Can-NonPay
Can-NonPay	cancel	--	Can-NonPay
Can-NonPay	PayTimerExpires	--	Can-NonPay
Can-Cust	giveInfo	--	Can-Cust
Can-Cust	payMoney	--	Can-Cust
Can-Cust	print	--	Can-Cust
Can-Cust	giveTicket	--	Can-Cust
Can-Cust	cancel	--	Can-Cust
Can-Cust	PayTimerExpires	--	Can-Cust

The advantage of a state-transition table is that it lists all possible state-transition combinations, not just the valid ones. When testing critical, high-risk systems such as avionics or medical devices, testing every state-transition pair may be required, including those that are not valid. In addition, creating a state-transition table often unearths combinations that were not identified, documented, or dealt with in the requirements. It is highly beneficial to discover these defects before coding begins.

■■■■■■■■■■■■■■■■■■
Key Point

The advantage of a state-transition table is that it lists all possible state-transition combinations, not just the valid ones.

Using a state-transition table can help detect defects in implementation that enable invalid paths from one state to another. The disadvantage of such tables is that they become very large very quickly as the number of states and events increases. In addition, the tables are generally sparse; that is, most of the cells are empty.

Creating Test Cases

Information in the state-transition diagrams can easily be used to create test cases. Four different levels of coverage can be defined:

1. Create a set of test cases such that **all states** are "visited" at least once under test. The set of three test cases shown below meets this requirement. Generally this is a weak level of test coverage.

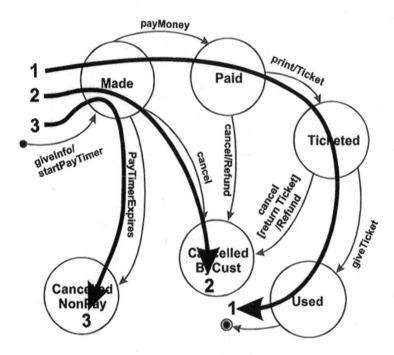

Figure 7-10

A set of test cases that "visit" each state.

2. Create a set of test cases such that **all events** are triggered at least once under test. Note that the test cases that cover each event can be the same as those that cover each state. Again, this is a weak level of coverage.

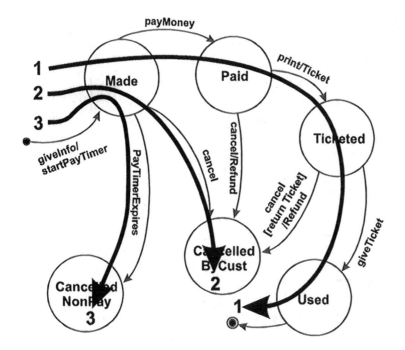

3. Create a set of test cases such that **all paths** are executed
    at least once under test. While this level is the most
    preferred because of its level of coverage, it may not be
    feasible. If the state-transition diagram has loops, then
    the number of possible paths may be infinite. For
    example, given a system with two states, A and B, where
    A transitions to B and B transitions to A. A few of the
    possible paths are:

    A→B
    A→B→A
    A→B→A→B→A→B
    A→B→A→B→A→B→A
    A→B→A→B→A→B→A→B→A→B
    ...

and so on forever. Testing of loops such as this can be important if they may result in accumulating computational errors or resource loss (locks without corresponding releases, memory leaks, etc.).

4. Create a set of test cases such that **all transitions** are exercised at least once under test. This level of testing provides a good level of coverage without generating large numbers of tests. This level is generally the one recommended.

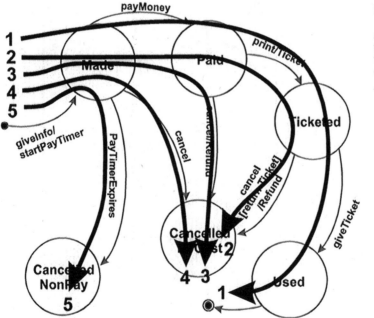

Test cases can also be read directly from the state-transition table. The gray rows in the following table show all the valid transitions.

Current State	Event	Action	Next State
null	giveInfo	startPayTimer	Made
null	payMoney	--	null
null	print	--	null
null	giveTicket	--	null
null	cancel	--	null
null	PayTimerExpires	--	null
Made	giveInfo	--	Made
Made	payMoney	--	Paid
Made	print	--	Made
Made	giveTicket	--	Made
Made	cancel	--	Can-Cust
Made	PayTimerExpires	--	Can-NonPay
Paid	giveInfo	--	Paid
Paid	payMoney	--	Paid
Paid	print	Ticket	Ticketed
Paid	giveTicket	--	Paid
Paid	cancel	Refund	Can-Cust
Paid	PayTimerExpires	--	Paid
Ticketed	giveInfo	--	Ticketed
Ticketed	payMoney	--	Ticketed
Ticketed	print	--	Ticketed
Ticketed	giveTicket	--	Used
Ticketed	cancel	Refund	Can-Cust
Ticketed	PayTimerExpires	--	Ticketed
Used	giveInfo	--	Used
Used	payMoney	--	Used
Used	print	--	Used
Used	giveTicket	--	Used
Used	cancel	--	Used
Used	PayTimerExpires	--	Used
Can-NonPay	giveInfo	--	Can-NonPay
Can-NonPay	payMoney	--	Can-NonPay
Can-NonPay	print	--	Can-NonPay
Can-NonPay	giveTicket	--	Can-NonPay
Can-NonPay	cancel	--	Can-NonPay
Can-NonPay	PayTimerExpires	--	Can-NonPay

■■■■■■■■■■■■■■■■■■

Table 7-2

Testing all valid transitions from a State-transition table.

Can-Cust	giveInfo	--	Can-Cust
Can-Cust	payMoney	--	Can-Cust
Can-Cust	print	--	Can-Cust
Can-Cust	giveTicket	--	Can-Cust
Can-Cust	cancel	--	Can-Cust
Can-Cust	PayTimerExpires	--	Can-Cust

In addition, depending on the system risk, you may want to create test cases for some or all of the invalid state/event pairs to make sure the system has not implemented invalid paths.

Applicability and Limitations

State-Transition diagrams are excellent tools to capture certain system requirements, namely those that describe states and their associated transitions. These diagrams then can be used to direct our testing efforts by identifying the states, events, and transitions that should be tested.

State-Transition diagrams are not applicable when the system has no state or does not need to respond to real-time events from outside of the system. An example is a payroll program that reads an employee's time record, computes pay, subtracts deductions, saves the record, prints a paycheck, and repeats the process.

Summary

- State-Transition diagrams direct our testing efforts by identifying the states, events, actions, and transitions that should be tested. Together, these define how a system interacts with the outside world, the events it processes, and the valid and invalid order of these events.

- A state-transition diagram is not the only way to document system behavior. They may be easier to comprehend, but state-transition tables may be easier to use in a complete and systematic manner.

- The generally recommended level of testing using state-transition diagrams is to create a set of test cases such that all transitions are exercised at least once under test. In high-risk systems, you may want to create even more test cases, approaching all paths if possible.

Practice

1. This exercise refers to the Stateless University Registration System Web site described in Appendix B. Below is a state-transition diagram for the "enroll in a course" and "drop a course" process. Determine a set of test cases that you feel adequately cover the enroll and drop process.

   The following terms are used in the diagram:

   Events
   > **create** – Create a new course.
   > **enroll** – Add a student to the course.
   > **drop** – Drop a student from the course.

   Attributes
   > **ID** – The student identification number.
   > **max** – The maximum number of students a course can hold.
   > **#enrolled** – The number of students currently enrolled in the course.

#waiting – The number of students currently on the Wait List for this course.

Tests

isEnrolled – Answers "is the student enrolled (on the Section List)?"

onWaitList – Answers "is the student on the WaitList?"

Lists

SectionList – A list of students enrolled in the class.

WaitList – A list of students waiting to be enrolled in a full class.

Symbols

++ Increment by 1.

-- Decrement by 1.

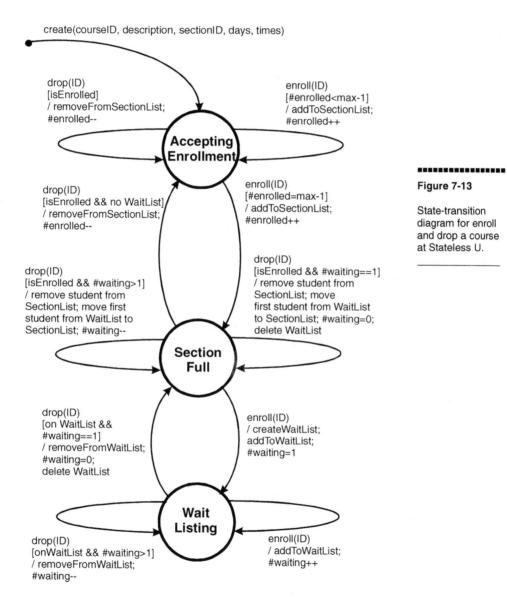

create(courseID, description, sectionID, days, times)

drop(ID)
[isEnrolled]
/ removeFromSectionList;
#enrolled--

enroll(ID)
[#enrolled<max-1]
/ addToSectionList;
#enrolled++

Accepting Enrollment

drop(ID)
[isEnrolled && no WaitList]
/ removeFromSectionList;
#enrolled--

enroll(ID)
[#enrolled=max-1]
/ addToSectionList;
#enrolled++

drop(ID)
[isEnrolled && #waiting>1]
/ remove student from
SectionList; move first
student from WaitList to
SectionList; #waiting--

drop(ID)
[isEnrolled && #waiting==1]
/ remove student from
SectionList; move
first student from WaitList
to SectionList; #waiting=0;
delete WaitList

Section Full

drop(ID)
[on WaitList &&
#waiting==1]
/ removeFromWaitList;
#waiting=0;
delete WaitList

enroll(ID)
/ createWaitList;
addToWaitList;
#waiting=1

Wait Listing

drop(ID)
[onWaitList && #waiting>1]
/ removeFromWaitList;
#waiting--

enroll(ID)
/ addToWaitList;
#waiting++

Figure 7-13

State-transition
diagram for enroll
and drop a course
at Stateless U.

References

Binder, Robert V. (1999). *Testing Object-Oriented Systems: Models, Patterns, and Tools*. Addison-Wesley.

Fowler, Martin and Kendall Scott (1999). *UML Distilled: A Brief Guide to the Standard Object Modeling Language (2nd Edition)*. Addison-Wesley.

Harel, David. "Statecharts: a visual formalism for complex systems." *Science of Computer Programming 8*, 1987, pp 231-274.

Mealy, G.H. "A method for synthesizing sequential circuits." *Bell System Technical Journal*, 34(5): 1045-1079, 1955.

Moore, E.F. "Gedanken-experiments on sequential machines," *Automata Studies* (C. E. Shannon and J. McCarthy, eds.), pp. 129–153, Princeton, New Jersey: Princeton University Press, 1956.

Rumbaugh, James, et al. (1991). *Object-Oriented Modeling and Design*. Prentice-Hall.

Chapter 8 –
Domain Analysis Testing

Standing in the concessions car of the Orient Express as it hissed and lurched away from the station, Special Agent Chu could feel enemy eyes watching him from the inky shadows and knew that he was being tested, for although he had never tasted a plug of tobacco in his life, he was impersonating an arms dealer known to be a connoisseur, so he knew that he, the Chosen One, Chow Chu, had no choice but to choose the choicest chew on the choo-choo.

— Loren Haarsma

Introduction

In the chapters on Equivalence Class and Boundary Value testing, we considered the testing of individual variables that took on values within specified ranges. In this chapter we will consider the testing of multiple variables simultaneously. There are two reasons to consider this:

- We rarely will have time to create test cases for every variable in our systems. There are simply too many.

- Often variables interact. The value of one variable constrains the acceptable values of another. In this case, certain defects cannot be discovered by testing them individually.

Domain analysis is a technique that can be used to identify efficient and effective test cases when multiple variables can or should be tested together. It builds on and generalizes equivalence class and boundary value testing to n simultaneous dimensions. Like those techniques, we are searching for situations where the boundary has been defined or implemented incorrectly.

In two dimensions (with two interacting parameters) the following defects can occur:

- A shifted boundary in which the boundary is displaced vertically or horizontally
- A tilted boundary in which the boundary is rotated at an incorrect angle
- A missing boundary
- An extra boundary

■■■■■■■■■■■■■■■■■■
Key Point

Domain analysis is a technique that can be used to identify efficient and effective test cases when multiple variables should be tested together.

Figure 8-1 is adapted from Binder. It illustrates these four types
of defects graphically.

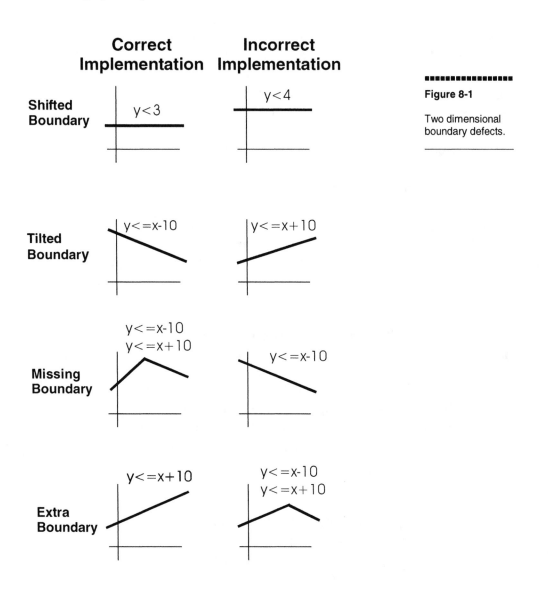

Figure 8-1

Two dimensional
boundary defects.

Certainly there can be interactions between three or more variables, but the diagrams are more difficult to visualize.

Technique

The domain analysis process guides us in choosing efficient and effective test cases. First, a number of definitions:

- An **on** point is a value that lies on a boundary.

- An **off** point is a value that does not lie on a boundary.

- An **in** point is a value that satisfies all the boundary conditions but does not lie on a boundary.

- An **out** point is a value that does not satisfy any boundary condition.

Choosing **on** and **off** points is more complicated that it may appear.

- When the boundary is closed (defined by an operator containing an equality, i.e., $\leq$, $\geq$, or $=$) so that points on the boundary are included in the domain, then an **on** point lies on the boundary and is included within the domain. An **off** point lies *outside* the domain.

- When the boundary is open (defined by an inequality operator $<$ or $>$) so that points on the boundary are not included in the domain, then an **on** point lies on the boundary but is not included within the domain. An **off** point lies *inside* the domain.

Confused? At this point examples are certainly in order.

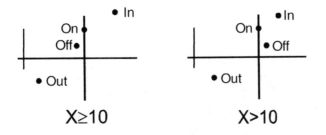

Figure 8-2

Examples of on, off, in, and out points for both closed and open boundaries.

On the left is an example of a closed boundary. The region defined consists of all the points greater than or equal to 10. The **on** point has the value 10. The **off** point is slightly off the boundary and *outside* the domain. The **in** point is within the domain. The **out** point is outside the domain.

On the right is an example of an open boundary. The region defined consists of all the points greater than (but not equal to) 10. Again, the **on** point has a value of 10. The **off** point is slightly off the boundary and *inside* the domain. The **in** point is within the domain. The **out** point is outside the domain.

Having defined these points, the 1x1 ("one-by-one") domain analysis technique instructs us to choose these test cases:

- For each relational condition (≥, >, ≤, or <) choose one **on** point and one **off** point.

- For each strict equality condition (=) choose one **on** point and two **off** points, one slightly less than the conditional value and one slightly greater than the value.

Note that there is no reason to repeat identical tests for adjacent domains. If an **off** point for one domain is the **in** point for another, do not duplicate these tests.

Binder suggests a very useful table for documenting 1x1 domain analysis test cases called the Domain Test Matrix.

Variable/ Condition Type			Test Cases														
			1	2	3	4	5	6	7	8	9	10	11	12	13	14	15	16
X1	C11	On																
		Off																
	C12	On																
		Off																
	...	On																
		Off																
	C1m	On																
		Off																
	Typical	In																
X2	C21	On																
		Off																
	C22	On																
		Off																
	...	On																
		Off																
	C2m	On																
		Off																
	Typical	In																
Expected Result																		

Note that test cases 1 through 8 test the **on** points and **off** points for each condition of the first variable (X1) while holding the value of the second variable (X2) at a typical **in** point. Test cases 9 through 16 hold the first variable at a typical **in** point while testing the **on** and **off** points for each condition of the second variable. Additional variables and conditions would follow the same pattern.

■■■■■■■■■■■■■■■■■

Table 8-1

Example Domain Test Matrix.

Example

Admission to Stateless University is made by considering a combination of high school grades and ACT test scores. The shaded cells in the following table indicate the combinations that would guarantee acceptance. Grade Point Averages (GPAs) are shown across the top while ACT scores are shown down the left side. Stateless University is a fairly exclusive school in terms of its admission policy.

Explanation

The ACT Assessment is an examination designed to assess high school students' general educational development and their ability to complete college-level work.

The Grade Point Average is based on converting letter grades to numeric values

A = 4.0 (Best)
B = 3.0
C = 2.0 (Average)
D = 1.0

Table 8-2

Stateless University Admissions Matrix.

		GPA						
		0.0 – 3.4	3.5	3.6	3.7	3.8	3.9	4.0
ACT Score	36		▓	▓	▓	▓	▓	▓
	35			▓	▓	▓	▓	▓
	34				▓	▓	▓	▓
	33					▓	▓	▓
	32						▓	▓
	31							▓
	0 - 30							

This table can be represented as the solution set of these three linear equations:

$$ACT \leq 36 \text{ (the highest score possible)}$$
$$GPA \leq 4.0 \text{ (the highest value possible)}$$
$$10*GPA + ACT \geq 71$$

(The third equation can be found by using the good old **y=mx+b** formula from elementary algebra. Use points {ACT=36, GPA=3.5} and {ACT=31, GPA=4.0} and crank—that's math slang for solve the pair of simultaneous equations obtained by substituting each of these two points into the **y=mx+b** equation.)

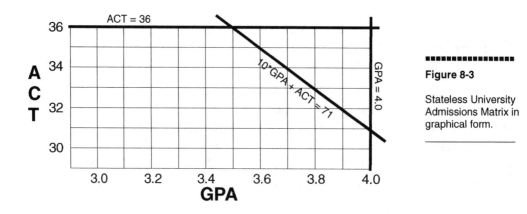

■■■■■■■■■■■■■■■■■

Figure 8-3

Stateless University
Admissions Matrix in
graphical form.

The following test cases cover these three boundaries using the
1x1 domain analysis process.

			1	2	3	4	5	6
GPA	GPA ≤	On	4.0					
	4.0	Off		4.1				
	Typical	In			3.7	3.8	3.8	3.9
ACT	ACT ≤	On			36			
	36	Off				37		
	Typical	In	34	33			32	35
GPA/ACT	10*GPA	On						
	+ ACT ≥ 71	Off						
	Typical	In	3.9/35	3.8/34	3.6/36	3.8/34	3.7/34	3.8/32
Expected Result			Admit	Reject	Admit	Reject	Admit	Reject

■■■■■■■■■■■■■■■■■

Table 8-3

1x1 Domain Analysis
test cases for
Stateless University
admissions.

Test cases 1 and 2 verify the GPA ≤ 4.0 constraint. Case 1
checks on the GPA = 4.0 boundary while case 2 checks just
outside the boundary with GPA = 4.1. Both of these cases use
typical values for the ACT and GPA/ACT constraints.

Test cases 3 and 4 verify the ACT ≤ 36 constraint. Case 3 checks
on the ACT = 36 boundary while case 4 checks just outside the

boundary with ACT = 37. Both of these cases use typical values for the GPA and GPA/ACT constraints.

Test cases 5 and 6 verify the $10*GPA + ACT \geq 71$ constraint. Case 5 checks on the GPA = 3.7 and ACT = 34 boundary while case 6 checks just outside the boundary with GPA=3.8 and ACT = 32. Both of these cases use typical values for the GPA and ACT constraints.

Applicability and Limitations

Domain analysis is applicable when multiple variables (such as input fields) should be tested together either for efficiency or because of a logical interaction. While this technique is best suited to numeric values, it can be generalized to Booleans, strings, enumerations, etc.

Summary

- Domain analysis facilitates the testing of multiple variables simultaneously. It is useful because we rarely will have time to create test cases for every variable in our systems. There are simply too many. In addition, often variables interact. When the value of one variable constrains the acceptable values of another, certain defects cannot be discovered by testing them individually.

- It builds on and generalizes equivalence class and boundary value testing to n simultaneous dimensions. Like those techniques, we are searching for situations where the boundary has been implemented incorrectly.

- In using the 1x1 domain analysis technique for each relational condition ($\geq$, $>$, $\leq$, or $<$) we choose one **on** point and one **off** point. For each strict equality condition ($=$) we choose one **on** point and two **off** points, one slightly less than the conditional value and one slightly greater than the value.

Practice

1. Stateless University prides itself in preparing not just educated students but good citizens of their nation. (That's what their advertising brochure says.) In addition to their major and minor coursework, Stateless U. requires each student to take (and pass) a number of General Education classes. These are:

   - College Algebra (the student may either take the course or show competency through testing).

   - Our Nation's Institutions—a survey course of our nation's history, government, and place in the world.

   - From four to sixteen hours of Social Science courses (numbers 100–299).

   - From four to sixteen hours of Physical Science courses (numbers 100–299)

   - No more than twenty-four combined hours of Social Science and Physical Science courses may be counted toward graduation.

Apply 1x1 domain analysis to these requirements, derive the test cases, and use Binder's Domain Test Matrix to document them.

References

Beizer, Boris (1990). *Software Testing Techniques*. Van Nostrand Reinhold.

Binder, Robert V. (2000). *Testing Object-Oriented Systems: Models, Patterns, and Tools*. Addison-Wesley.

Chapter 9 –
Use Case Testing

The Insect Keeper General, sitting astride his giant hovering aphid, surveyed the battlefield which reeked with the stench of decay and resonated with the low drone of the tattered and dying mutant swarms as their legs kicked forlornly at the sky before turning to his master and saying, 'My Lord, your flies are undone.'

— Andrew Vincent

Introduction

Up until now we have examined test case design techniques for parts of a system—input variables with their ranges and boundaries, business rules as represented in decision tables, and system behaviors as represented in state-transition diagrams. Now it is time to consider test cases that exercise a system's functionalities from start to finish by testing each of its individual transactions.

Defining the transactions that a system processes is a vital part of the requirements definition process. Various approaches to documenting these transactions have been used in the past. Examples include flowcharts, HIPO diagrams, and text. Today, the most popular approach is the use case diagram. Like decision tables and state-transition diagrams, use cases are usually created by developers for developers. But, like these other techniques, use cases hold a wealth of information useful to testers.

Use cases were created by Ivar Jacobsen and popularized in his book *Object-Oriented Software Engineering: A Use Case Driven Approach*. Jacobsen defines a "use case" as a scenario that describes the use of a system by an actor to accomplish a specific goal. By "actor" we mean a user, playing a role with respect to the system, seeking to use the system to accomplish something worthwhile within a particular context. Actors are generally people although other systems may also be actors. A "scenario" is a sequence of steps that describe the interactions between the actor and the system. Note that the use case is defined from the perspective of the user, not the system. Note also that the internal workings of the system, while vital, are not part of the use case definition. The set of use cases makes up the functional requirements of a system.

The Unified Modeling Language notion for use cases is:

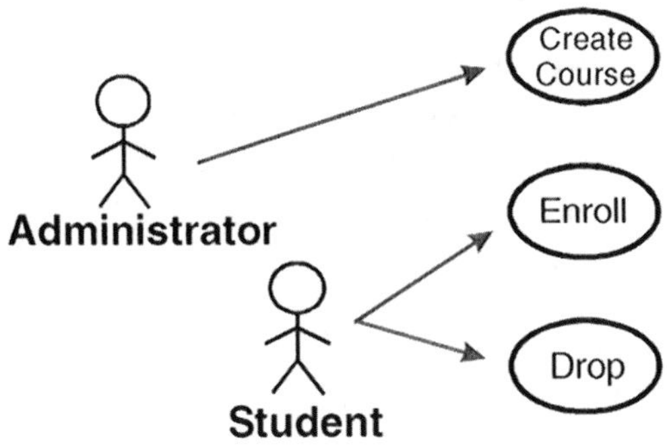

Figure 9-1

Some Stateless University use cases.

The stick figures represent the actors, the ellipses represent the use cases, and the arrows show which actors initiate which use cases.

It is important to note that while use cases were created in the context of object-oriented systems development, they are equally useful in defining functional requirements in other development paradigms as well.

The value of use cases is that they:

- Capture the system's functional requirements from the user's perspective; not from a technical perspective, and irrespective of the development paradigm to be used.

- Can be used to actively involve users in the requirements gathering and definition process.

- Provide the basis for identifying a system's key internal components, structures, databases, and relationships.

- Serve as the foundation for developing test cases at the system and acceptance level.

Technique

Unfortunately, the level of detail specified in the use cases is not sufficient, either for developers or testers. In his book *Writing Effective Use Cases,* Alistair Cockburn has proposed a detailed template for describing use cases. The following is adapted from his work:

Use Case Component	Description	
Use Case Number or Identifier	A unique identifier for this use case	
Use Case Name	The name should be the goal stated as a short active verb phrase	
Goal in Context	A more detailed statement of the goal if necessary	
Scope	Corporate | System | Subsystem	
Level	Summary | Primary task | Subfunction	
Primary Actor	Role name or description of the primary actor	
Preconditions	The required state of the system before the use case is triggered	
Success End Conditions	The state of the system upon successful completion of this use case	
Failed End Conditions	The state of the system if the use case cannot execute to completion	
Trigger	The action that initiates the execution of the use case	
Main Success Scenario	Step	Action
	1	
	2	

■■■■■■■■■■■■■■■■■
Table 9-1

Use case template.

	...	
Extensions	Conditions under which the main success scenario will vary and a description of those variations	
Sub-Variations	Variations that do not affect the main flow but that must be considered	
Priority	Criticality	
Response Time	Time available to execute this use case	
Frequency	How often this use case is executed	
Channels to Primary Actor	Interactive | File | Database | ...	
Secondary Actors	Other actors needed to accomplish this use case	
Channels to Secondary Actors	Interactive | File | Database | ...	
Date Due	Schedule information	
Completeness Level	Use Case identified (0.1)| Main scenario defined (0.5) | All extensions defined (0.8) | All fields complete (1.0)	
Open Issues	Unresolved issues awaiting decisions	

Example

Consider the following example from the Stateless University Registration System. A student wants to register for a course using SU's online registration system, SURS.

Use Case Component	Description		
Use Case Number or Identifier	SURS1138		
Use Case Name	Register for a course (a class taught by a faculty member)		
Goal in Context			
Scope	System		
Level	Primary task		
Primary Actor	Student		
Preconditions	None		
Success End Conditions	The student is registered for the course—the course has been added to the student's course list		
Failed End Conditions	The student's course list is unchanged		
Trigger	Student selects a course and "Registers"		
Main Success Scenario **A: Actor** **S: System**	**Step**	**Action**	
	1	A: Selects "Register for a course"	
	2	A: Selects course (e.g. Math 1060)	
	3	S: Displays course description	
	4	A: Selects section (Mon & Wed 9:00am)	
	5	S: Displays section days and times	
	6	A: Accepts	
	7	S: Adds course/section to student's course list	

▪▪▪▪▪▪▪▪▪▪▪▪▪▪▪▪▪▪

Table 9-2

Example use case.

Extensions	2a	Course does not exist S: Display message and exit
	4a	Section does not exist S: Display message and exit
	4b	Section is full S: Display message and exit
	6a	Student does not accept S: Display message and exit
Sub-Variations	Student may use - Web - Phone	
Priority	Critical	
Response Time	10 seconds or less	
Frequency	Approximately 5 courses x 10,000 students over a 4-week period	
Channels to Primary Actor	Interactive	
Secondary Actors	None	
Channels to Secondary Actors	N/A	
Date Due	1 Feb	
Completeness Level	0.5	
Open Issues	None	

Hopefully each use case has been through an inspection process before it was implemented. To test the implementation, the basic rule is to create at least one test case for the main success scenario and at least one test case for each extension.

Because use cases do not specify input data, the tester must select it. Typically we use the equivalence class and boundary value techniques described earlier. Also a Domain Test Matrix (see the Domain Analysis Testing chapter for an example) may be a useful way of documenting the test cases.

It is important to consider the risk of the transaction and its variants under test. Less risky transactions merit less testing. More risky transactions should receive more testing. For them consider the following approach.

To create test cases, start with normal data for the most often used transactions. Then move to boundary values and invalid data. Next, choose transactions that, while not used often, are vital to the success of the system (i.e., **Shut Down The Nuclear Reactor**). Make sure you have at least one test case for every Extension in the use case. Try transactions in strange orders. Violate the preconditions (if that can happen in actual use). If a transaction has loops, don't just loop through once or twice—be diabolical. Look for the longest, most convoluted path through the transaction and try it. If transactions should be executed in some logical order, try a different order. Instead of entering data top-down, try bottom-up. Create "goofy" test cases. If you don't try strange things, you know the users will.

Most paths through a transaction are easy to create. They correspond to valid and invalid data being entered. More difficult are those paths due to some kind of exceptional condition—low memory, disk full, connection lost, driver not loaded, etc. It can be very time consuming for the tester to create or simulate these conditions. Fortunately, a tool is available to help the tester

■■■■■■■■■■■■■■■■■
Key Point

Always remember to evaluate the risk of each use case and extension and create test cases accordingly.

■■■■■■■■■■■■■■■■■
Free Stuff

Download Holodeck from http://www.sisecure.com/holodeck/holodeck-trial.aspx.

simulate these problems—Holodeck, created by James Whittaker and his associates at Florida Institute of Technology. Holodeck monitors the interactions between an application and its operating system. It logs each system call and enables the tester to simulate a failure of any call at will. In this way, the disk can be "made full," network connections can "become disconnected," data transmission can "be garbled," and a host of other problems can be simulated.

A major component of transaction testing is test data. Boris Beizer suggests that 30 percent to 40 percent of the effort in transaction testing is generating, capturing, or extracting test data. Don't forget to include resources (time and people) for this work in your project's budget.

■■■■■■■■■■■■■■■■■
Note

One testing group designates a "data czar" whose sole responsibility is to provide test data.

Applicability and Limitations

Transaction testing is generally the cornerstone of system and acceptance testing. It should be used whenever system transactions are well defined. If system transactions are not well defined, you might consider polishing up your resume or C.V.

While creating at least one test case for the main success scenario and at least one for each extension provides some level of test coverage, it is clear that, no matter how much we try, most input combinations will remain untested. Do not be overconfident about the quality of the system at this point.

Summary

- A use case is a scenario that describes the use of a system by an actor to accomplish a specific goal. An "actor" is a user, playing a role with respect to the system, seeking to use the system to accomplish something worthwhile within a particular context. A scenario is a sequence of steps that describe the interactions between the actor and the system.

- A major component of transaction testing is test data. Boris Beizer suggests that 30 percent to 40 percent of the effort in transaction testing is generating, capturing, or extracting test data. Don't forget to include resources (time and people) for this work in your project's budget.

- While creating at least one test case for the main success scenario and at least one for each extension provides some level of test coverage, it is clear that, no matter how much we try, most input combinations will remain untested. Do not be overconfident about the quality of the system at this point.

Practice

1. Given the "Register For A Course" use case for the Stateless University Registration System described previously, create a set of test cases so that the main success scenario and each of the extensions are tested at least once. Choose "interesting" test data using the equivalence class and boundary value techniques.

References

Beizer, Boris (1990). *Software Testing Techniques* (Second Edition). Van Nostrand Reinhold.

Beizer, Boris (1995). *Black-Box Testing: Techniques for Functional Testing of Software and Systems*. John Wiley & Sons.

Cockburn, Alistair (2000). *Writing Effective Use Cases*. Addison-Wesley.

Fowler, Martin and Kendall Scott (1999). *UML Distilled: A Brief Guide to the Standard Object Modeling Language (2nd Edition)*. Addison-Wesley.

Jacobsen, Ivar, et al. (1992). *Object-Oriented Systems Engineering: A Use Case Driven Approach*. Addison-Wesley.

Section II –
White Box Testing
Techniques

Definition

White box testing is a strategy in which testing is based on the internal paths, structure, and implementation of the software under test (SUT). Unlike its complement, black box testing, white box testing generally requires detailed programming skills.

The general white box testing process is:

- The SUT's implementation is analyzed.
- Paths through the SUT are identified.
- Inputs are chosen to cause the SUT to execute selected paths. This is called path sensitization. Expected results for those inputs are determined.
- The tests are run.
- Actual outputs are compared with the expected outputs.
- A determination is made as to the proper functioning of the SUT.

Applicability

White box testing can be applied at all levels of system development—unit, integration, and system. Generally white box testing is equated with unit testing performed by developers. While this is correct, it is a narrow view of white box testing.

White box testing is more than code testing—it is **path** testing. Generally, the paths that are tested are within a module (unit testing). But we can apply the same techniques to test paths between modules within subsystems, between subsystems within systems, and even between entire systems.

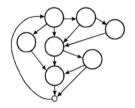

Disadvantages

White box testing has four distinct disadvantages. First, the number of execution paths may be so large than they cannot all be tested. Attempting to test all execution paths through white box testing is generally as infeasible as testing all input data combinations through black box testing.

Second, the test cases chosen may not detect data sensitivity errors. For example:

p=q/r;

may execute correctly except when r=0.

$y=2*x$ // should read $y=x^2$

will pass for test cases x=0, y=0 and x=2, y=4

Third, white box testing assumes the control flow is correct (or very close to correct). Since the tests are based on the existing paths, nonexistent paths cannot be discovered through white box testing.

Fourth, the tester must have the programming skills to understand and evaluate the software under test. Unfortunately, many testers today do not have this background.

Advantages

When using white box testing, the tester can be sure that every path through the software under test has been identified and tested.

Chapter 10 –
Control Flow Testing

It was from the primeval wellspring of an antediluvian passion that my story arises which, like the round earth flattened on a map, is but a linear projection of an otherwise periphrastic and polyphiloprogenitive, non-planar, non-didactic, self-inverting construction whose obscurantist geotropic liminality is beyond reasonable doubt.

— Milinda Banerjee

Introduction

Control flow testing is one of two white box testing techniques. This testing approach identifies the execution paths through a module of program code and then creates and executes test cases to cover those paths. The second technique, discussed in the next chapter, focuses on data flow.

Unfortunately, in any reasonably interesting module, attempting exhaustive testing of all control flow paths has a number of significant drawbacks.

- The number of paths could be huge and thus untestable within a reasonable amount of time. Every decision doubles the number of paths and every loop multiplies the paths by the number of iterations through the loop. For example:

  ```
  for (i=1; i<=1000; i++)
    for (j=1; j<=1000; j++)
      for (k=1; k<=1000; k++)
        doSomethingWith(i,j,k);
  ```

  executes doSomethingWith() one billion times (1000 x 1000 x 1000). Each unique path deserves to be tested.

- Paths called for in the specification may simply be missing from the module. Any testing approach based on implemented paths will never find paths that were not implemented.

■■■■■■■■■■■■■■■■■■

Key Point

Path: A sequence of statement execution that begins at an entry and ends at an exit.

```
if (a>0) doIsGreater();
if (a==0) doIsEqual();
// missing statement – if (a<0) doIsLess();
```

- Defects may exist in processing statements within the module even through the control flow itself is correct.

```
// actual (but incorrect) code
a=a+1;
// correct code
a=a-1;
```

- The module may execute correctly for almost all data values but fail for a few.

```
int blech (int a, int b) {
    return a/b;
}
```

fails if **b** has the value 0 but executes correctly if **b** is not 0.

Even though control flow testing has a number of drawbacks, it is still a vital tool in the tester's toolbox.

Technique

Control Flow Graphs

Control flow graphs are the foundation of control flow testing. These graphs document the module's control structure. Modules of code are converted to graphs, the paths through the graphs are analyzed, and test cases are created from that analysis. Control flow graphs consist of a number of elements:

■■■■■■■■■■■■■■■■■

Key Point

Control flow graphs are the foundation of control flow testing.
_____

Process Blocks

A process block is a sequence of program statements that execute sequentially from beginning to end. No entry into the block is permitted except at the beginning. No exit from the block is permitted except at the end. Once the block is initiated, every statement within it will be executed sequentially. Process blocks are represented in control flow graphs by a bubble with one entry and one exit.

Decision Point

A decision point is a point in the module at which the control flow can change. Most decision points are binary and are implemented by **if-then-else** statements. Multi-way decision points are implemented by case statements. They are represented by a bubble with one entry and multiple exits.

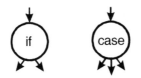

Junction Point

A junction point is a point at which control flows join together.

The following code example is represented by its associated flow graph:

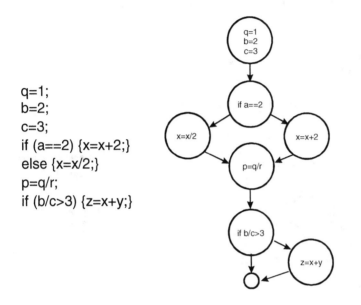

```
q=1;
b=2;
c=3;
if (a==2) {x=x+2;}
else {x=x/2;}
p=q/r;
if (b/c>3) {z=x+y;}
```

Figure 10-1

Flow graph
equivalent of
program code.

Levels of Coverage

In control flow testing, different levels of test coverage are
defined. By "coverage" we mean the percentage of the code that
has been tested vs. that which is there to test. In control flow
testing we define coverage at a number of different levels. (Note
that these coverage levels are not presented in order. This is
because, in some cases, it is easier to define a higher coverage
level and then define a lower coverage level in terms of the
higher.)

Level 1

The lowest coverage level is "100% statement coverage"
(sometimes the "100%" is dropped and is referred to as
"statement coverage"). This means that every statement
within the module is executed, under test, at least once.
While this may seem like a reasonable goal, many

defects may be missed with this level of coverage. Consider the following code snippet:

```
if (a>0) {x=x+1;}
if (b==3) {y=0;}
```

This code can be represented in graphical form as:

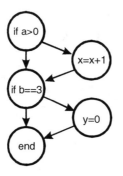

Figure 10-2

Graphical representation of the two-line code snippet.

These two lines of code implement four different paths of execution:

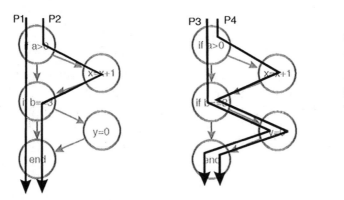

Figure 10-3

Four execution paths.

While a single test case is sufficient to test every line of code in this module (for example, use a=6 and b=3 as input), it is apparent that this level of coverage will miss testing many paths. Thus, statement coverage, while a beginning, is generally not an acceptable level of testing.

Even though statement coverage is the lowest level of coverage, even that may be difficult to achieve in practice. Often modules have code that is executed only in exceptional circumstances—low memory, full disk, unreadable files, lost connections, etc. Testers may find it difficult or even impossible to simulate these circumstances and thus code that deals with these problems will remain untested.

Holodeck is a tool that can simulate many of these exceptional situations. According to Holodeck's specification it "will allow you, the tester, to test software by observing the system calls that it makes and create test cases that you may use during software execution to modify the behavior of the application. Modifications might include manipulating the parameters sent to functions or changing the return values of functions within your software. In addition, you may also set error-codes and other system events. This set of possibilities allows you to emulate environments that your software might encounter - hence the name 'Holodeck.' Instead of needing to unplug your network connection, create a disk with bad sectors, corrupt packets on the network, or perform any outside or special manipulation of your machine, you can use Holodeck to emulate these problems. Faults can easily be placed into any software testing project that you are using with Holodeck."

■■■■■■■■■■■■■■■■■■■

Holodeck

To download Holodeck visit http://www.sisecure.com/holodeck/holodeck-trial.aspx.

Level 0

Actually, there is a level of coverage below "100% statement coverage." That level is defined as "test whatever you test; let the users test the rest." The corporate landscape is strewn with the sun-bleached bones of organizations who have used this testing approach. Regarding this level of coverage, Boris Beizer wrote "testing less than this [100% statement coverage] for new software is unconscionable and should be criminalized. ... In case I haven't made myself clear, ... untested code in a system is stupid, shortsighted, and irresponsible."

Level 2

The next level of control flow coverage is "100% decision coverage." This is also called "branch coverage." At this level enough test cases are written so that each decision that has a **TRUE** and **FALSE** outcome is evaluated at least once. In the previous example this can be achieved with two test cases (a=2, b=2 and a=4, b=3).

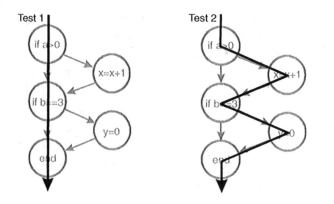

■■■■■■■■■■■■■■■■■

Figure 10-4

Two test cases that yield 100% decision coverage.

Case statements with multiple exits would have tests for each exit. Note that decision coverage does not necessarily guarantee path coverage but it does guarantee statement coverage.

Level 3

Not all conditional statements are as simple as the ones previously shown. Consider these more complicated statements:

```
if (a>0 && c==1) {x=x+1;}
if (b==3 || d<0) {y=0;}
```

To be **TRUE**, the first statement requires **a** greater than 0 **and c** equal 1. The second requires **b** equal 3 **or d** less than 0.

In the first statement if the value of **a** were set to 0 for testing purposes then the **c==1** part of the condition would not be tested. (In most programming languages the second expression would not even be evaluated.) The next level of control flow coverage is "100% condition coverage." At this level enough test cases are written so that each condition that has a **TRUE** and **FALSE** outcome that makes up a decision is evaluated at least once. This level of coverage can be achieved with two test cases (**a>0, c=1, b=3, d<0** and **a≤0, c≠1, b≠3, d≥0**). Condition coverage is usually better than decision coverage because every individual condition is tested at least once while decision coverage can be achieved without testing every condition.

Level 4

Consider this situation:

```
if(x&&y) {conditionedStatement;}
// note: && indicates logical AND
```

We can achieve condition coverage with two test cases (**x=TRUE, y=FALSE** and **x=FALSE, y=TRUE**) but note that with these choices of data values the conditionedStatement will never be executed. Given the possible combination of conditions such as these, to be more complete "100% decision/condition" coverage can be selected. At this level test cases are created for every condition and every decision.

Level 5

To be even more thorough, consider how the programming language compiler actually evaluates the multiple conditions in a decision. Use that knowledge to create test cases yielding "100% multiple condition coverage."

```
if (a>0 && c==1) {x=x+1;}
if (b==3 || d<0) {y=0;}
// note: || means logical OR
```

will be evaluated as:

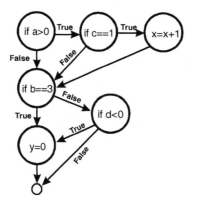

■■■■■■■■■■■■■■■■■■
Figure 10-5

Compiler evaluation of complex conditions.

This level of coverage can be achieved with four test cases:

a>0, c=1, b=3, d<0
a≤0, c=1, b=3, d≥0
a>0, c≠1, b≠3, d<0
a≤0, c≠1, b≠3, d≥0

Achieving 100% multiple condition coverage also achieves decision coverage, condition coverage, and decision/condition coverage. Note that multiple condition coverage does not guarantee path coverage.

Level 7

Finally we reach the highest level, which is "100% path coverage." For code modules without loops the number of paths is generally small enough that a test case can actually be constructed for each path. For modules with loops, the number of paths can be enormous and thus pose an intractable testing problem.

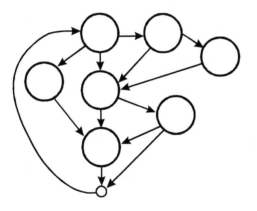

Figure 10-6

An interesting flow diagram with many, many paths.

Level 6

When a module has loops in the code paths such that the number of paths is infinite, a significant but meaningful reduction can be made by limiting loop execution to a small number of cases. The first case is to execute the loop zero times; the second is to execute the loop one time, the third is to execute the loop n times where n is a small number representing a typical loop value; the fourth is to execute the loop its maximum number of times m. In addition you might try $m-1$ and $m+1$.

Before beginning control flow testing, an appropriate level of coverage should be chosen.

Structured Testing / Basis Path Testing

No discussion on control flow testing would be complete without a presentation of structured testing, also known as basis path testing. Structured testing is based on the pioneering work of Tom McCabe. It uses an analysis of the topology of the control flow graph to identify test cases.

The structured testing process consists of the following steps:
- Derive the control flow graph from the software module.
- Compute the graph's Cyclomatic Complexity (C).
- Select a set of C basis paths.
- Create a test case for each basis path.
- Execute these tests.

Consider the following control flow graph:

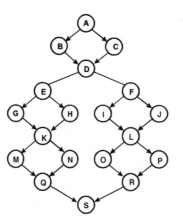

■■■■■■■■■■■■■■■■■
Figure 10-7

An example control flow graph.

McCabe defines the Cyclomatic Complexity (C) of a graph as

$$C = edges - nodes + 2$$

Edges are the arrows, and nodes are the bubbles on the graph. The preceding graph has 24 edges and 19 nodes for a Cyclomatic Complexity of 24-19+2 = 7.

In some cases this computation can be simplified. If all decisions in the graph are binary (they have exactly two edges flowing out), and there are p binary decisions, then

$$C = p+1$$

Cyclomatic Complexity is exactly the minimum number of independent, nonlooping paths (called basis paths) that can, in linear combination, generate all possible paths through the module. In terms of a flow graph, each basis path traverses at least one edge that no other path does.

McCabe's structured testing technique calls for creating C test cases, one for each basis path.

Because the set of basis paths covers all the edges and nodes of the control flow graph, satisfying this structured testing criteria automatically guarantees both branch and statement coverage.

A process for creating a set of basis paths is given by McCabe:

1. Pick a "baseline" path. This path should be a reasonably "typical" path of execution rather than an exception processing path. The best choice would be the most important path from the tester's view.

■■■■■■■■■■■■■■■■■
IMPORTANT !

Creating and executing C test cases, based on the basis paths, guarantees both branch and statement coverage.

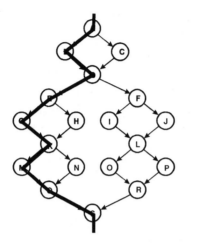

■■■■■■■■■■■■■■■■■■

Figure 10-8

The chosen
baseline basis path
ABDEGKMQS

2. To choose the next path, change the outcome of the first decision along the baseline path while keeping the maximum number of other decisions the same as the baseline path.

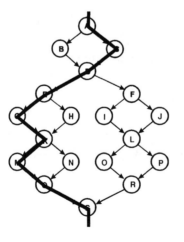

■■■■■■■■■■■■■■■■■■

Figure 10-9

The second basis
path
ACDEGKMQS

3. To generate the third path, begin again with the baseline but vary the second decision rather than the first.

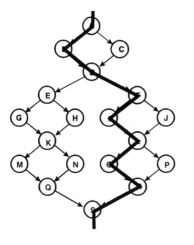

Figure 10-10

The third basis path
ABDFILORS

4. To generate the fourth path, begin again with the baseline but vary the third decision rather than the second. Continue varying each decision, one by one, until the bottom of the graph is reached.

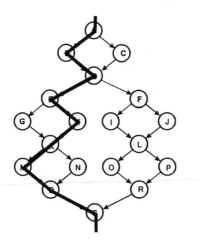

Figure 10-11

The fourth basis path
ABDEHKMQS

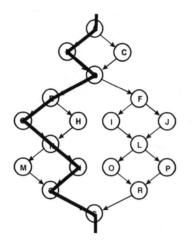

■■■■■■■■■■■■■■■■■■

Figure 10-12

The fifth basis path
ABDEGKNQS

5. Now that all decisions along the baseline path have been flipped, we proceed to the second path, flipping its decisions, one by one. This pattern is continued until the basis path set is complete.

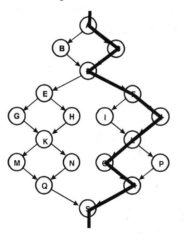

■■■■■■■■■■■■■■■■■■

Figure 10-13

The sixth basis path
ACDFJLORS

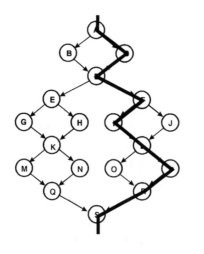

■■■■■■■■■■■■■■■■■■

Figure 10-14

The seventh basis
path
ACDFILPRS
_____

Thus, a set of basis paths for this graph are:

ABDEGKMQS
ACDEGKMQS
ABDFILORS
ABDEHKMQS
ABDEGKNQS
ACDFJLORS
ACDFILPRS

Structured testing calls for the creation of a test case for each of these paths. This set of test cases will guarantee both statement and branch coverage.

Note that multiple sets of basis paths can be created that are not necessarily unique. Each set, however, has the property that a set of test cases based on it will execute every statement and every branch.

Example

Consider the following example from Brown & Donaldson. It is the code that determines whether B&D should buy or sell a particular stock. Unfortunately, the inner workings are a highly classified trade secret so the actual processing code has been removed and generic statements like s1; s2; etc. have substituted for them. The control flow statements have been left intact but their actual conditions have been removed and generic conditions like c1 and c2 have been put in their place. (You didn't think we'd really show you how to know whether to buy or sell stocks, did you?)

■■■■■■■■■■■■■■■■■
Note

s1, s2, ... represent
Java statements
while c1, c2, ...
represent
conditions.

```
boolean evaluateBuySell (TickerSymbol ts) {
s1;
s2;
s3;
if (c1) {s4; s5; s6;}
else {s7; s8;}
while (c2) {
    s9;
    s10;
    switch (c3) {
        case-A:
            s20;
            s21;
            s22;
            break; // End of Case-A
        case-B:
            s30;
            s31;
            if (c4) {
                s32;
                s33;
                s34;
            }
            else {
                s35;
            }
```

■■■■■■■■■■■■■■■■■
Figure 10-15

Java code for
Brown &
Donaldson's
evaluateBuySell
module.

```
            break; // End of Case-B
        case-C:
            s40;
            s41;
            break; // End of Case-C
        case-D:
            s50;
            break; // End of Case-D
        } // End Switch
    s60;
    s61;
    s62;
    if (c5) {s70; s71; }
    s80;
    s81;
} // End While
s90;
s91;
s92;
return result;
```

The following flow diagram corresponds to this Java code:

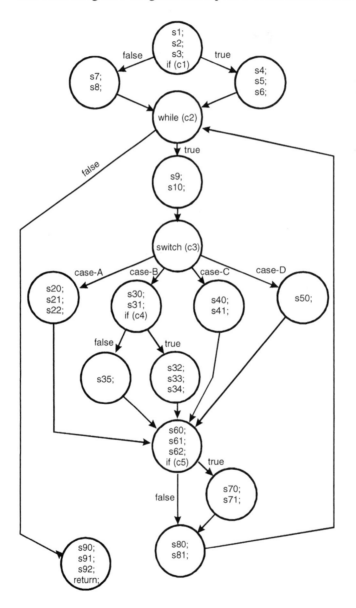

Figure 10-16

Control flow graph for Brown & Donaldson's evaluateBuySell module.

The cyclomatic complexity of this diagram is computed by

$$edges - nodes + 2$$
or
$$22\text{-}16\text{+}2 = 8$$

Let's remove the code and label each node for simplicity in describing the paths.

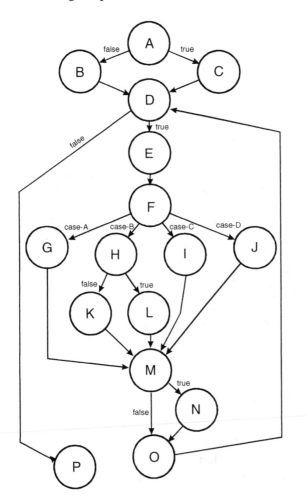

Figure 10-17

Control flow graph for Brown & Donaldson's evaluateBuySell module.

A set of eight basis paths is:

1. ABDP
2. ACDP
3. ABDEFGMODP
4. ABDEFHKMODP
5. ABDEFIMODP
6. ABDEFJMODP
7. ABDEFHLMODP
8. ABDEFIMNODP

Remember that basis path sets are not unique; there can be multiple sets of basis paths for a graph.

This basis path set is now implemented as test cases. Choose values for the conditions that would sensitize each path and execute the tests.

Test Case	C1	C2	C3	C4	C5
1	False	False	N/A	N/A	N/A
2	True	False	N/A	N/A	N/A
3	False	True	A	N/A	False
4	False	True	B	False	False
5	False	True	C	N/A	False
6	False	True	D	N/A	False
7	False	True	B	True	False
8	False	True	C	N/A	True

■■■■■■■■■■■■■■■■■

Table 10-1

Data values to sensitize the different control flow paths.

Applicability and Limitations

Control flow testing is the cornerstone of unit testing. It should be used for all modules of code that cannot be tested sufficiently through reviews and inspections. Its limitations are that the tester must have sufficient programming skill to understand the code and its control flow. In addition, control flow testing can be very time consuming because of all the modules and basis paths that comprise a system.

Summary

- Control flow testing identifies the execution paths through a module of program code and then creates and executes test cases to cover those paths.

- Control flow graphs are the foundation of control flow testing. Modules of code are converted to graphs, the paths through the graphs are analyzed, and test cases are created from that analysis.

- Cyclomatic Complexity is exactly the minimum number of independent, nonlooping paths (called basis paths) that can, in linear combination, generate all possible paths through the module.

- Because the set of basis paths covers all the edges and nodes of the control flow graph, satisfying this structured testing criteria automatically guarantees both branch and statement coverage.

Practice

1. Below is a brief program listing. Create the control flow diagram, determine its Cyclomatic Complexity, choose a set of basis paths, and determine the necessary values for the conditions to sensitize each path.

```
if (c1) {
    while (c2) {
        if (c3) { s1; s2;
            if (c5) s5;
            else s6;
            break; // Skip to end of while
        else
        if (c4) { }
        else { s3; s4; break; }
    } // End of while
} // End of if
s7;
if (c6) s8; s9;
s10;
```

References

Beizer, Boris (1990). *Software Testing Techniques* (Second Edition). Van Nostrand Reinhold.

Myers, Glenford (1979). *The Art of Software Testing*. John Wiley & Sons.

Pressman, Roger S. (1982). *Software Engineering: A Practitioner's Approach* (Fourth Edition). McGraw-Hill.

Watson, Arthur H. and Thomas J. McCabe. *Structured Testing: A Testing Methodology Using the Cyclomatic Complexity Metric*. NIST Special Publication 500-235 available at http://www.mccabe.com/nist/nist_pub.php

Chapter 11 –
Data Flow Testing

Holly had reached the age and level of maturity to comprehend the emotional nuances of Thomas Wolfe's assertion "you can't go home again," but in her case it was even more poignant because there was no home to return to: her parents had separated, sold the house, euthanized Bowser, and disowned Holly for dropping out of high school to marry that 43-year-old manager of Trailer Town in Idaho—and even their trailer wasn't a place she could call home because it was only a summer sublet.

— Eileen Ostrow Feldman

Introduction

A lmost every programmer has made this type of mistake:

```
main() {
int x;
if (x==42) { ...}
}
```

The mistake is referencing the value of a variable without first assigning a value to it. Naive developers unconsciously assume that the language compiler or run-time system will set all variables to zero, blanks, **TRUE**, 42, or whatever they require later in the program. A simple C program that illustrates this defect is:

```
#include <stdio.h>
main() {
int x;
printf ("%d",x);
}
```

The value printed will be whatever value was "left over" in the memory location to which x has been assigned, not necessarily what the programmer wanted or expected.

Data flow testing is a powerful tool to detect just such errors. Rapps and Weyuker, popularizers of this approach, wrote, "It is our belief that, just as one would not feel confident about a program without executing every statement in it as part of some test, one should not feel confident about a program without having seen the effect of using the value produced by each and every computation."

■■■■■■■■■■■■■■■■■
Key Point

Data flow testing is a powerful tool to detect improper use of data values due to coding errors.

Technique

Variables that contain data values have a defined life cycle. They are created, they are used, and they are killed (destroyed). In some programming languages (FORTRAN and BASIC, for example) creation and destruction are automatic. A variable is created the first time it is assigned a value and destroyed when the program exits.

In other languages (like C, C++, and Java) the creation is formal. Variables are declared by statements such as:

```
int x;      // x is created as an integer
string y;  // y is created as a string
```

These declarations generally occur within a block of code beginning with an opening brace { and ending with a closing brace }. Variables defined within a block are created when their definitions are executed and are automatically destroyed at the end of a block. This is called the "scope" of the variable. For example:

```
{          // begin outer block
 int x;    // x is defined as an integer within this outer block
 ...;      // x can be accessed here
  {        // begin inner block
 int y;   // y is defined within this inner block
  ...;     // both x and y can be accessed here
  }        // y is automatically destroyed at the end of
          // this block
  ...;     // x can still be accessed, but y is gone
}   // x is automatically destroyed
```

Variables can be used in computation (a=b+1). They can also be used in conditionals (if (a>42)). In both uses it is equally important that the variable has been assigned a value before it is used.

Three possibilities exist for the first occurrence of a variable through a program path:

1. ~d the variable does not exist (indicated by the ~),
    then it is defined (d)
2. ~u the variable does not exist, then it is used (u)
3. ~k the variable does not exist, then it is killed
    or destroyed (k)

The first is correct. The variable does not exist and then it is defined. The second is incorrect. A variable must not be used before it is defined. The third is probably incorrect. Destroying a variable before it is created is indicative of a programming error.

Now consider the following time-sequenced pairs of defined (d), used (u), and killed (k):

dd	Defined and defined again—not invalid but suspicious. Probably a programming error.
du	Defined and used—perfectly correct. The normal case.
dk	Defined and then killed—not invalid but probably a programming error.
ud	Used and defined—acceptable.
uu	Used and used again—acceptable.
uk	Used and killed—acceptable.
kd	Killed and defined—acceptable. A variable is killed and then redefined.
ku	Killed and used—a serious defect. Using a variable that does not exist or is undefined is always an error.
kk	Killed and killed—probably a programming error.

■■■■■■■■■■■■■■■■■
Key Point

Examine time-sequenced pairs of defined, used, and killed variable references.

A data flow graph is similar to a control flow graph in that it shows the processing flow through a module. In addition, it details the definition, use, and destruction of each of the module's variables. We will construct these diagrams and verify that the define-use-kill patterns are appropriate. First, we will perform a static test of the diagram. By "static" we mean we examine the diagram (formally through inspections or informally through look-sees). Second, we perform dynamic tests on the module. By "dynamic" we mean we construct and execute test cases. Let's begin with the static testing.

Static Data Flow Testing

The following control flow diagram has been annotated with define-use-kill information for each of the variables used in the module.

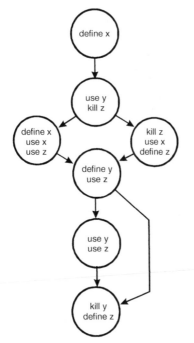

■■■■■■■■■■■■■■■■■
Figure 11-1

The control flow diagram annotated with define-use-kill information for each of the module's variables.

For each variable within the module we will examine define-use-kill patterns along the control flow paths. Consider variable x as we traverse the left and then the right path:

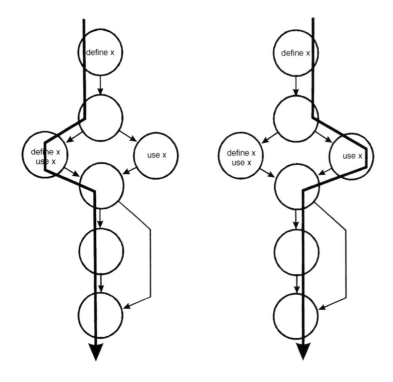

■■■■■■■■■■■■■■■■■■

Figure 11-2

The control flow diagram annotated with define-use-kill information for the x variable.

The define-use-kill patterns for x (taken in pairs as we follow the paths) are:

~define	correct, the normal case
define-define	suspicious, perhaps a programming error
define-use	correct, the normal case

Now for variable y. Note that the first branch in the module has no impact on the y variable.

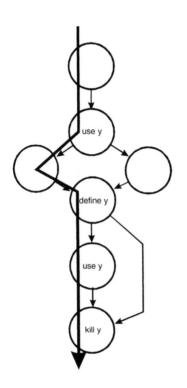

Figure 11-3

The control flow diagram annotated with define-use-kill information for the y variable.

The define-use-kill patterns for y (taken in pairs as we follow the paths) are:

~use	major blunder
use-define	acceptable
define-use	correct, the normal case
use-kill	acceptable
define-kill	probable programming error

Now for variable z.

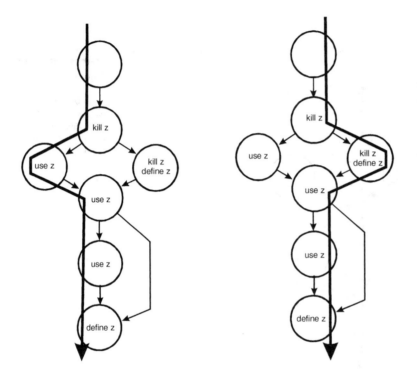

The define-use-kill patterns (taken in pairs as we follow the paths) are:

~kill	programming error
kill-use	major blunder
use-use	correct, the normal case
use-define	acceptable
kill-kill	probably a programming error
kill-define	acceptable
define-use	correct, the normal case

In performing a static analysis on this data flow model the following problems have been discovered:

x: define-define
y: ~use
y: define-kill
z: ~kill
z: kill-use
z: kill-kill

Unfortunately, while static testing can detect many data flow errors, it cannot find them all. Consider the following situations:

1. Arrays are collections of data elements that share the same name and type. For example

    int stuff[100];

    defines an array named stuff consisting of 100 integer elements. In C, C++, and Java the individual elements are named stuff[0], stuff[1], stuff[2], etc. Arrays are defined and destroyed as a unit but specific elements of the array are used individually. Often programmers refer to stuff[j] where j changes dynamically as the program executes. In the general case, static analysis cannot determine whether the define-use-kill rules have been followed properly unless each element is considered individually.

2. In complex control flows it is possible that a certain path can never be executed. In this case an improper define-use-kill combination might exist but will never be executed and so is not truly improper.

3. In systems that process interrupts, some of the define-use-kill actions may occur at the interrupt level while other define-use-kill actions occur at the main processing level. In addition, if the system uses multiple levels of execution priorities, static analysis of the myriad of possible interactions is simply too difficult to perform manually.

For this reason, we now turn to dynamic data flow testing.

Dynamic Data Flow Testing

Because data flow testing is based on a module's control flow, it assumes that the control flow is basically correct. The data flow testing process is to choose enough test cases so that:

- Every "define" is traced to each of its "uses"
- Every "use" is traced from its corresponding "define"

To do this, enumerate the paths through the module. This is done using the same approach as in control flow testing: Begin at the module's entry point, take the leftmost path through the module to its exit. Return to the beginning and vary the first branching condition. Follow that path to the exit. Return to the beginning and vary the second branching condition, then the third, and so on until all the paths are listed. Then, for every variable, create at least one test case to cover every define-use pair.

Applicability and Limitations

Data flow testing builds on and expands control flow testing techniques. As with control flow testing, it should be used for all modules of code that cannot be tested sufficiently through reviews and inspections. Its limitations are that the tester must have sufficient programming skill to understand the code, its control flow, and its variables. Like control flow testing, data flow testing can be very time consuming because of all the modules, paths, and variables that comprise a system.

Summary

- A common programming mistake is referencing the value of a variable without first assigning a value to it.

- A data flow graph is similar to a control flow graph in that it shows the processing flow through a module. In addition, it details the definition, use, and destruction of each of the module's variables. We will use these diagrams to verify that the define-use-kill patterns are appropriate.

- Enumerate the paths through the module. Then, for every variable, create at least one test case to cover every define-use pair.

Practice

1. The following module of code computes n! (n factorial) given a value for n. Create data flow test cases covering each variable in this module. Remember, a single test case can cover a number of variables.

```
int factorial (int n) {
        int answer, counter;
        answer = 1;
        counter = 1;

loop:
```

```
                if (counter > n) return answer;
                answer = answer * counter;
                counter = counter + 1;
                goto loop;
        }
```

2. Diagram the control flow paths and derive the data flow
   test cases for the following module:

```
int module( int selector) {
int foo, bar;
switch selector {
case SELECT-1:
        foo = calc_foo_method_1();
        break;
case SELECT-2:
        foo = calc_foo_method_2();
        break;
case SELECT-3:
        foo = calc_foo_method_3();
        break;
        }
switch foo {
case FOO-1:
        bar = calc_bar_method_1();
        break;
case FOO-2:
        bar = calc_bar_method_2();
        break;
        }
return foo/bar;
}
```

Do you have any concerns with this code? How would
you deal with them?

References

Beizer, Boris (1990). *Software Testing Techniques.* Van Nostrand Reinhold.

Binder, Robert V. (2000). *Testing Object-Oriented Systems: Models, Patterns, and Tools.* Addison-Wesley.

Marick, Brian (1995). *The Craft of Software Testing: Subsystem Testing Including Object-Based and Object-Oriented Testing.* Prentice-Hall.

Rapps, Sandra and Elaine J. Weyuker. "Data Flow Analysis Techniques for Test Data Selection." Sixth International Conference on Software Engineering, Tokyo, Japan, September 13–16, 1982.

Section III –
Testing Paradigms

Paradigms

In his book, *Paradigms: The Business of Discovering the Future*, Joel Barker defines a paradigm as "a set of rules and regulations (written or unwritten) that does two things: (1) it establishes or defines boundaries, and (2) it tells you how to behave inside the boundaries in order to be successful." Futurist Marilyn Ferguson sees a paradigm as "a framework of thought … a scheme for understanding and explaining certain aspects of reality."

Paradigms are useful because they help us make sense of the complexities of the world around us. In this way, paradigms sharpen our vision. But paradigms can blind us to realities. Paradigms act as psychological filters. Data that does not match our paradigms is blocked. In this way, paradigms cloud our vision.

In software testing today, two very different paradigms are battling for adherents—scripted testing and exploratory testing.

Scripted testing is based on the sequential examination of requirements, followed by the design and documentation of test cases, followed by the execution of those test cases. The scripted tester's motto is, "Plan your work, work your plan."

Exploratory testing is a very different paradigm. Rather than a sequential approach, exploratory testing emphasizes *simultaneous* learning, test design, and test execution. The tester designs and executes tests while exploring the product.

The next two chapters describe these paradigms. A word of warning though—each paradigm is described at the extreme end of the process spectrum. Rarely will either paradigm be used as inflexibly as described. More often, scripted testing may be

■■■■■■■■■■■■■■■■■
Word Of Warning !

In the following chapters the scripted and exploratory paradigms are defined at the extreme ends of the spectrum. Rarely will either be used as inflexibly as described.

somewhat exploratory and exploratory testing may be somewhat scripted.

Test Planning

Planning has been defined as simply "figuring out what to do next." To be most effective and efficient, planning is important. But when and how should that planning be done? Scripted testing emphasizes the value of early test design as a method of detecting requirements and design defects before the code is written and the system put into production. Its focus is on accountability and repeatability. Exploratory testing challenges the idea that tests must be designed so very early in the project, when our knowledge is typically at its minimum. Its focus is on learning and adaptability.

References

Barker, Joel Arthur (1992). *Paradigms: The Business of Discovering the Future.* HarperCollins.

Ferguson, Marilyn (1980). *The Aquarian Conspiracy: Personal and Social Transformation in Our Time.* Putnam Publishing Group.

Chapter 12 –
Scripted Testing

Jane was toast, and not the light buttery kind, nay, she was the kind that's been charred and blackened in the bottom of the toaster and has to be thrown away because no matter how much of the burnt part you scrape off with a knife, there's always more blackened toast beneath, the kind that not even starving birds in winter will eat, that kind of toast.

— Beth Knutson

Introduction

For scripted testing to be understood, it must be understood in its historical context. Scripted testing emerged as one of the component parts of the Waterfall model of software development. The Waterfall model defines a number of sequential development phases with specific entry and exit criteria, tasks to be performed, and deliverables (tangible work products) to be created. It is a classic example of the "plan your work, work your plan" philosophy. Typical Waterfall phases include:

1. System Requirements – Gathering the requirements for the system.
2. Software Requirements – Gathering the requirements for the software portion of the system.
3. Requirements Analysis – Analyzing, categorizing, and refining the software requirements.
4. Program Design – Choosing architectures, modules, and interfaces that define the system.
5. Coding – Writing the programming code that implements the design.
6. Testing – Evaluating whether the requirements were properly understood (Validation) and the design properly implemented by the code (Verification).
7. Operations – Put the system into production.

This model was first described in 1970 in a paper entitled "Managing the Development of Large Scale Systems" by Dr. Winston W. Royce. Royce drew the following diagram showing the relationships between development phases:

■■■■■■■■■■■■■■■■■■
Interesting Trivia

A Google search for "plan your work" and "work your plan" found 3,570 matches including:

- Football recruiting
- Business planning
- Building with concrete blocks
- Online marketing
- Industrial distribution
- The Princeton University's Women's Water Polo Team
- And thousands more

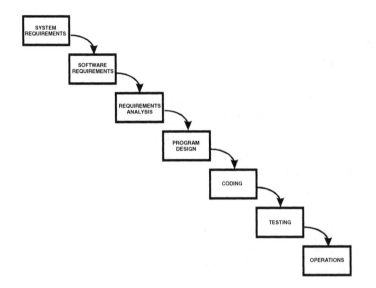

What process was used before Waterfall? It is a process known as "Code & Fix." Programmers simply coded. Slogans like "Requirements? Requirements? We don't need no stinkin' Requirements!" hung on the walls of programmers' offices. Development was like the scene in the movie *Raiders of the Lost Ark*. Our hero, Indiana Jones, is hiding from the bad guys. Indy says, "I'm going to get that truck." Marion, our heroine, turns to him and asks, "How are you going to get that truck?" Indy replies, "I don't know. I'm making this up as I go." If we substituted "build that system" for "get that truck" we'd have the way real men and real women built software systems in the good old days.

Today we take a different view of scripted testing. Any development methodology along the spectrum from Waterfall to Rapid Application Development (RAD) may use scripted testing. Whenever repeatability, objectivity, and auditability are important, scripted testing can be used.

■■■■■■■■■■■■■■■■

Curious Historical Note

Today, Winston Royce is known as the father of the Waterfall model of software development. In fact, in his paper he was actually proposing an iterative and incremental process that included early prototyping – something many organizations are just now discovering.

Repeatability means that there is a definition of a test (from design through to detailed procedure) at a level of detail sufficient for someone other than the author to execute it in an identical way. Objectivity means that the test creation does not depend on the extrordinary (near magical) skill of the person creating the test but is based on well understood test design principles. Auditability includes traceability from requirements, design, and code to the test cases and back again. This enables formal measures of testing coverage.

"Plan your work, work your plan." No phrase so epitomizes the scripted testing approach as does this one, and no document so epitomizes the scripted testing approach as does IEEE Std 829-1998, the "IEEE Standard for Software Test Documentation."

This standard defines eight documents that can be used in software testing. These documents are:

- Test plan
- Test design specification
- Test case specification
- Test procedure specification
- Test item transmittal report
- Test log
- Test incident report
- Test summary report

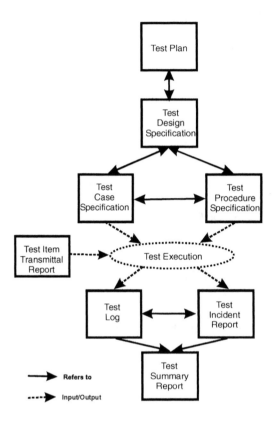

■■■■■■■■■■■■■■■■■■

Figure 12-2

The IEEE 829 Test Documents

Figure 12-2 shows the relationships between these documents. Note that the first four documents that define the test plan, test designs, and test cases are all created before the product is developed and the actual testing is begun. This is a key idea in scripted testing—plan the tests based on the formal system requirements.

Curiously, the IEEE 829 standard states, "This standard specifies the form and content of individual test documents. It does not specify the required set of test documents." In other words, the standard does not require you to create any of the documents described. That choice is left to you as a tester, or to your organization. But, the standard requires that if you choose to write a test plan, test case specification, etc., that document must follow the IEEE 829 standard.

The IEEE 829 standard lists these advantages for its use:

- "A standardized test document can facilitate communication by providing a common frame of reference.

- The content definition of a standardized test document can serve as a completeness checklist for the associated testing process.

- A standardized set can also provide a baseline for the evaluation of current test documentation practices.

- The use of these documents significantly increases the manageability of testing. Increased manageability results from the greatly increased visibility of each phase of the testing process."

IEEE 829 Document Descriptions

The IEEE 829 standard defines eight different documents. Each document is composed of a number of sections.

Test Plan

The purpose of the test plan is to describe the scope, approach, resources, and schedule of the testing activities. It describes the items (components) and features (functionality, performance, security, usability, etc.) to be tested, tasks to be performed, deliverables (tangible work products) to be created, testing responsibilities, schedules, and approvals required. Test plans can be created at the project level (master test plan) or at subsidiary levels (unit, integration, system, acceptance, etc.). The test plan is composed of the following sections:

1. Test plan identifier – A unique identifier so that this document can be distinguished from all other documents.
2. Introduction – A summary of the software to be tested. A brief description and history may be included to set the context. References to other relevant documents useful for understanding the test plan are appropriate. Definitions of unfamiliar terms may be included.
3. Test items – Identifies the software items that are to be tested. The word "item" is purposely vague. It is a "chunk" of software that is the object of testing.
4. Features to be tested – Identifies the characteristics of the items to be tested. These include functionality, performance, security, portability, usability, etc.
5. Features not to be tested – Identifies characteristics of the items that will not be tested and the reasons why.
6. Approach – The overall approach to testing that will ensure that all items and their features will be adequately tested.
7. Item pass/fail criteria – The criteria used to determine whether each test item has passed or failed testing.
8. Suspension criteria and resumption requirements – The conditions under which testing will be suspended and the subsequent conditions under which testing will be resumed.
9. Test deliverables – Identifies the documents that will be created as a part of the testing process.
10. Testing tasks – Identifies the tasks necessary to perform the testing.

11. Environmental needs – Specifies the environment required to perform the testing including hardware, software, communications, facilities, tools, people, etc.
12. Responsibilities – Identifies the people/groups responsible for executing the testing tasks.
13. Staffing and training needs – Specifies the number and types of people required to perform the testing, including the skills needed.
14. Schedule – Defines the important key milestones and dates in the testing process.
15. Risks and contingencies – Identifies high-risk assumptions of the testing plan. Specifies prevention and mitigation plans for each.
16. Approvals – Specifies the names and titles of each person who must approve the plan.

Test Design Specification

The purpose of the test design specification is to identify a set of features to be tested and to describe a group of test cases that will adequately test those features. In addition, refinements to the approach listed in the test plan may be specified. The test design specification is composed of the following sections:

1. Test design specification identifier – A unique identifier so that this document can be distinguished from all other documents.
2. Features to be tested – Identifies the test items and the features that are the object of this test design specification.
3. Approach refinements – Specifies the test techniques to be used for this test design.
4. Test identification – Lists the test cases associated with this test design. Provides a unique identifier and a short description for each test case.

5. Feature pass/fail criteria – The criteria used to determine whether each feature has passed or failed testing.

Test Case Specification

The purpose of the test case specification is to specify in detail each test case listed in the test design specification. The test case specification is composed of the following sections:

1. Test case specification identifier – A unique identifier so that this document can be distinguished from all other documents.
2. Test items – Identifies the items and features to be tested by this test case.
3. Input specifications – Specifies each input required by this test case.
4. Output specifications – Specifies each output expected after executing this test case.
5. Environmental needs – Any special hardware, software, facilities, etc. required for the execution of this test case that were not listed in its associated test design specification.
6. Special procedural requirements – Defines any special setup, execution, or cleanup procedures unique to this test case.
7. Intercase dependencies – Lists any test cases that must be executed prior to this test case.

Test Procedure Specification

The purpose of the test procedure specification is to specify the steps for executing a test case and the process for determining whether the software passed or failed the test. The test procedure specification is composed of the following sections:

1. Test procedure specification identifier – A unique identifier so that this document can be distinguished from all other documents.
2. Purpose – Describes the purpose of the test procedure and its corresponding test cases.
3. Special requirements – Lists any special requirements for the execution of this test procedure.
4. Procedure steps – Lists the steps of the procedure. Possible steps include: Set up, Start, Proceed, Measure, Shut Down, Restart, Stop, and Wrap Up.

Test Item Transmittal Report (a.k.a. Release Notes)

The purpose of the test item transmittal report is to specify the test items being provided for testing. The test item transmittal report is composed of the following sections:

1. Transmittal report identifier – A unique identifier so that this document can be distinguished from all other documents.
2. Transmitted items – Lists the items being transmitted for testing including their version or revision level.
3. Location – Identifies the location of the transmitted items.
4. Status – Describes the status of the items being transmitted. Include any deviations from the item's specifications.
5. Approvals – Specifies the names and titles of all persons who must approve this transmittal.

Test Log

The purpose of the test log is to provide a chronological record about relevant details observed during the test execution. The test log is composed of the following sections:

1. Test log identifier – A unique identifier so that this document can be distinguished from all other documents.
2. Description – Identifies the items being tested and the environment under which the test was performed.
3. Activity and event entries – For each event, lists the beginning and ending date and time, a brief description of the test execution, the results of the test, and unique environmental information, anomalous events observed, and the incident report identifier if an incident was logged.

Test Incident Report (a.k.a. Bug Report)

The purpose of the test incident report is to document any event observed during testing that requires further investigation. The test incident report is composed of the following sections:

1. Test incident report identifier – A unique identifier so that this document can be distinguished from all other documents.
2. Summary – Summarizes the incident.
3. Incident description – Describes the incident in terms of inputs, expected results, actual results, environment, attempts to repeat, etc.
4. Impact – Describes the impact this incident will have on other test plans, test design specifications, test procedures, and test case specifications. Also describes, if known, the impact this incident will have on further testing.

Test Summary Report

The purpose of the test summary report is to summarize the results of the testing activities and to provide an evaluation based on these results. The test summary report is composed of the following sections:

1. Test summary report identifier – A unique identifier (imagine that!) so that this document can be distinguished from all other documents.
2. Summary – Summarizes the evaluation of the test items.
3. Variance – Reports any variances from the expected results.
4. Comprehensive assessment – Evaluates the overall comprehensiveness of the testing process itself against criteria specified in the test plan.
5. Summary of results – Summarizes the results of the testing. Identifies all unresolved incidents.
6. Evaluation – Provides an overall evaluation of each test item including its limitations.
7. Summary of activities – Summarizes the major testing activities by task and resource usage.
8. Approvals – Specifies the names and titles of each person who must approve the report.

Advantages of Scripted Testing

1. Scripted testing provides a division of labor—planning, test case design, test case implementation, and test case execution that can be performed by people with specific skills and at different times during the development process.

2. Test design techniques such as equivalence class partitioning, boundary value testing, control flow testing, pairwise testing, etc. can be integrated into a formal testing process description that not only guides our testing but that could also be used to audit for process compliance.

3. Because scripted tests are created from requirements, design, and code, all important attributes of the system will be covered by tests and this coverage can be demonstrated.

4. Because the test cases can be traced back to their respective requirements, design, and code, coverage can be clearly defined and measured.

5. Because the tests are documented, they can be easily understood and repeated when necessary without additional test analysis or design effort.

6. Because the tests are defined in detail, they are more easily automated.

7. Because the tests are created early in the development process, this may free up additional time during the critical test execution period.

8. In situations where a good requirements specification is lacking, the test cases, at the end of the project, become the de facto requirements specification, including the results that demonstrate which requirements were actually fulfilled and which were not.

9. Scripted tests, when written to the appropriate level of detail, can be run by people who would otherwise not be

able to test the system because of lack of domain knowledge or lack of testing knowledge.

10. You may have special contractual requirements that can only be met by scripted testing.

11. There may be certain tests that must be executed in just the same way, every time, in order to serve as a kind of benchmark.

12. By creating the tests early in the project we can discover what we don't know.

13. By creating the tests early we can focus on the "big picture."

In his book *Software System Testing and Quality Assurance*, Boris Beizer summarizes in this way:

> "Testing is like playing pool. There's real pool and kiddie pool. In kiddie pool, you hit the balls and whatever pocket they happen to fall into, you claim as the intended pocket. It's not much of a game and although suitable to ten-year-olds it's hardly a challenge. The object of real pool is to specify the pocket in advance. Similarly for testing. There's real testing and kiddie testing. In kiddie testing, the tester says, after the fact, that the observed outcome was the intended outcome. In real testing the outcome is predicted and documented before the test is run."

Disadvantages of Scripted Testing

1. Scripted testing is very dependent on the quality of the system's requirements. Will the requirements really be

complete, consistent, unambiguous, and stable enough as the foundation for scripted testing? Perhaps not.

2.   Scripted testing is, by definition, inflexible. It follows the script. If, while testing, we see something curious, we note it in a Test Incident Report but we do not pursue it. Why not? Because it is not in the script to do so. Many interesting defects could be missed with this approach.

3.   Scripted testing is often used to "de-skill" the job of testing. The approach seems to be, "Teach a tester a skill or two and send them off to document mountains of tests. The sheer bulk of the tests will probably find most of the defects."

Summary

- "Plan your work, work your plan." Like the Waterfall model, no phrase so epitomizes the scripted testing approach as does this one, and no document so epitomizes the scripted testing approach as does IEEE Std 829-1998, the "IEEE Standard for Software Test Documentation."

- The IEEE Standard 829 defines eight documents that can be used in software testing. These documents are: test plan, test design specification, test case specification, test procedure specification, test item transmittal report, test log, test incident report, and test summary report.

- The advantages of scripted testing include formal documentation, coverage, and traceability.

References

Beizer, Boris (1984). *Software System Testing and Quality Assurance*. Van Nostrand Reinhold.

"IEEE Standard for Software Test Documentation," IEEE Std 829-1998. The Institute of Electrical and Electronics Engineers, Inc.
ISBN 0-7381-1443-X

Royce, Winston W. "Managing the Development of Large Software Systems," *Proceedings of the 9th International Conference on Software Engineering,* Monterey, CA, IEEE Computer Society Press, Los Alamitos, CA, 1987.
http://www.ipd.bth.se/uodds/pd&agile/royce.pdf

Chapter 13 –
Exploratory Testing

As she contemplated the setting sun, its dying rays casting the last of their brilliant purple light on the red-gold waters of the lake, Debbie realized that she should never again buy her sunglasses from a guy parked by the side of the road.

— Malinda Lingwall

Introduction

The term "exploratory testing," coined by Cem Kaner in his book *Testing Computer Software,* refers to an approach to testing that is very different from scripted testing. Rather than a sequential examination of requirements, followed by the design and documentation of test cases, followed by the execution of those test cases, exploratory testing, as defined by James Bach, is "*simultaneous* learning, test design, and test execution." The tester designs and executes tests while exploring the product.

In an article for StickyMinds.com entitled "Exploratory Testing and the Planning Myth," Bach wrote, "Exploratory Testing, as I practice it, usually proceeds according to a conscious plan. But not a rigorous plan … it's not scripted in detail." James adds, "Rigor requires certainty and implies completeness, but I perform exploratory testing precisely because there's so much I don't know about the product and I know my testing can never be fully complete." James continues, "To the extent that the next test we do is influenced by the result of the last test we did, we are doing exploratory testing. We become more exploratory when we can't tell what tests should be run, in advance of the test cycle."

In exploratory testing, the tester controls the design of test cases **as** they are performed rather than days, weeks, or even months before. In addition, the information the tester gains from executing a set of tests then guides the tester in designing and executing the next set of tests.

Note this process is called exploratory testing to distinguish it from ad hoc testing which (by my definition, although others may disagree) often denotes sloppy, careless, unfocused, random, and unskilled testing. Anyone, no matter what their

■■■■■■■■■■■■■■■■■
**Exploratory
Testing**

To the extent that the next test we do is influenced by the result of the last test we did, we are doing exploratory testing. We become more exploratory when we can't tell what tests should be run, in advance of the test cycle.

experience or skill level, can do ad hoc testing. That kind of testing is ineffective against all but the most defect-ridden systems, and even then may not find a substantial portion of the defects.

Bach suggests that in today's topsy-turvy world of incomplete, rapidly changing requirements and minimal time for testing, the classical sequential approach of Test Analysis followed by Test Design followed by Test Creation followed by Test Execution is like playing the game of "Twenty Questions" by writing out all the questions in advance. Consider the following discussion from a testing seminar discussing exploratory testing:

> **Instructor:** Let's play a game called "Twenty Questions." I am thinking about something in the universe. I'm giving you, the class, twenty questions to identify what I'm thinking about. Each question must be phrased in a way that it can be answered "Yes" or "No." (If I let you phrase the question in any form you could ask "What are you thinking about" and we would then call this game "One Question.") Ready? Brian, let's begin with you.
>
> **Brian:** Does it have anything to do with software testing?
>
> **Instructor:** No, that would be too easy.
>
> **Michael:** Is it large?
>
> **Instructor:** No, it's not large.
>
> **Rebecca:** Is it an animal?
>
> **Instructor:** No.
>
> **Rayanne:** Is it a plant?
>
> **Instructor:** Yes, it is a plant.
>
> **Henry:** Is it a tree?
>
> **Instructor:** No, it is not a tree.
>
> **Sree:** Is it big?
>
> **Instructor:** No, I've already said it is not large.
>
> **Eric:** Is it green?

■■■■■■■■■■■■■■■■■
Twenty Questions: The Game

A game in which one person thinks of something and others ask up to 20 questions to determine what has been selected. The questions must be answerable "Yes" or "No."

When played well, each question is based on the previous questions and their answers. Writing the questions out in advance prevents using the knowledge acquired from each answer.

Instructor: Yes, it is green.
Cheryl: Does it have leaves?
Instructor: Yes, it has leaves.
Galina: Is it an outdoor plant?
Instructor: Yes, it generally grows outdoors.
Jae: Is it a flowering plant?
Instructor: No, I don't believe so but I'm not a botanist.
Melanie: Is it a shrub?
Instructor: No.
Patrick: Is it a cactus?
Instructor: No, it is not a cactus.
Angel: Is it a cucumber?
Instructor: No, perhaps rather than guessing individual plants it would be more effective to identify categories.
Sundari: Is it a weed?
Instructor: No, good try though.
Lynn: Is it a perennial?
Instructor: No, I don't believe so. I think it must be replanted each year.
Julie: Does it grow from bulbs?
Instructor: No.
Michelle: Is it in everyone's yard?
Instructor: No, at least it's not in mine.
Kristie: Is it illegal? (Laughter in the class)
Instructor: No, it's quite legal. Well, we've gone through the class once. Brian, let's go back to you.
Brian: Is it poisonous?
Instructor: No, although my children think so.
Michael: Is it eaten?
Instructor: Yes, it is eaten.
Rebecca: Is it lettuce?
Instructor: No, not lettuce.
Rayanne: Is it spinach?
Instructor: Yes, it is spinach. Very good.

How successful would we be at this game if we had to write out all the questions in advance? When we play this game well, each question depends on the previous questions and their answers. So it is in exploratory testing. Each test provides us with information about the product. We may see evidence of the product's correctness; we may see evidence of its defects. We may see things that are curious; we're not sure what they mean, things that we wonder about and want to explore further. So, as we practice exploratory testing, we concurrently learn the product, design the tests, and execute these tests.

Description

In his classic time management book, *How to Get Control of Your Time and Your Life*, Alan Lakein suggests we should constantly ask ourselves: What is the most important thing I can do with my time right now? Exploratory testers ask an equivalent question: What is the most important test I can perform right now?

■■■■■■■■■■■■■■■■■
Key Question

What is the most important test I can perform right now?

A possible exploratory testing process is:

- Creating a conjecture (a mental model) of the proper functioning of the system
- Designing one or more tests that would disprove the conjecture
- Executing these tests and observing the outcomes
- Evaluating the outcomes against the conjecture
- Repeating this process until the conjecture is proved or disproved

Another process might be simply to explore and learn before forming conjectures of proper behavior.

Exploratory testing can be done within a "timebox," an uninterrupted block of time devoted to testing. These are typically between sixty and 120 minutes in length. This is long enough to perform solid testing but short enough so that the tester does not mentally wander. In addition, a timebox of this length is typically easier to schedule, easier to control, and easier to report.

When performing "chartered exploratory testing," a charter is first created to guide the tester within the timebox. This charter defines a clear mission for the testing session. The charter may define:

- What to test
- What documents (requirements, design, user manual, etc.) are available to the tester
- What tactics to use
- What kinds of defects to look for
- What risks are involved

This charter is a guideline to be used, **not** a script to be followed. Because of this approach, exploratory testing makes full use of the skills of testers. Bach writes, "The more we can make testing intellectually rich and fluid, the more likely we will hit upon the right tests at the right time."

■■■■■■■■■■■■■■■■■
Key Point

The charter is a guideline to be used, not a script to be followed.

Charters focus the exploratory tester's efforts within the timebox. Possible charters include:

- Thoroughly investigate a specific system function
- Define and then examine the system's workflows
- Identify and verify all the claims made in the user manual
- Understand the performance characteristics of the software
- Ensure that all input fields are properly validated

- Force all error conditions to verify each error message
- Check the design against user interface standards

It is possible to perform exploratory testing without a charter. This is called "freestyle exploratory testing." In this process testers use their skills to the utmost as they concurrently learn the product and design and execute tests.

Exploratory testers are skilled testers. (Of course, we want testers to be skilled no matter what testing process we are using!) The exploratory testing approach respects those skills and, in fact, depends on them. Good exploratory testers are:

- Good modelers, able to create mental models of the system and its proper behavior.
- Careful observers, able to see, hear, read, and comprehend.
- Skilled test designers, able to choose appropriate test design techniques in each situation. Bach emphasizes, "An exploratory tester is first and foremost a test designer."
- Able to evaluate risk and let it guide their testing.
- Critical thinkers, able to generate diverse ideas, integrate their observations, skills, and experiences to concurrently explore the product, design the tests, and execute the tests.
- Careful reporters, able to rigorously and effectively report to others what they have observed.
- Self managed, able to take the lead in testing rather than execute a plan devised by others.
- Not distracted by trivial matters.

Testers without these skills can still perform useful exploratory testing if they are properly supervised and coached.

In general, processes that have weak, slow, or nonexistent feedback mechanisms often do not perform well. Scripted testing is a prime example of a slow feedback loop. Exploratory testing provides a tight feedback loop between both test design and test execution. In addition, it provides tight feedback between testers and developers regarding the quality of the product being tested.

Advantages of Exploratory Testing

1. Exploratory testing is valuable in situations where choosing the next test case to be run cannot be determined in advance, but should be based on previous tests and their results.

2. Exploratory testing is useful when you are asked to provide rapid feedback on a product's quality on short notice, with little time, off the top of your head, when requirements are vague or even nonexistent, or early in the development process when the system may be unstable.

3. Exploratory testing is useful when, once a defect is detected, we want to explore the size, scope, and variations of that defect to provide better feedback to our developers.

4. Exploratory testing is a useful addition to scripted testing when the scripted tests become "tired," that is, they are not detecting many errors.

Disadvantages of Exploratory Testing

1. Exploratory testing has no ability to prevent defects. Because the design of scripted test cases begins during the requirements gathering and design phases, defects can be identified and corrected earlier.

2. If you are already sure exactly which tests must be executed, and in which order, there is no need to explore. Write and then execute scripted tests.

3. If you are required by contract, rule, or regulation to use scripted testing then do so. Consider adding exploratory tests as a complementary technique.

Summary

- Exploratory testing is defined as *"simultaneous* learning, test design, and test execution." The tester designs and executes tests while exploring the product.

- In exploratory testing, the tester controls the design of test cases **as** they are performed rather than days, weeks, or even months before. In addition, the information the tester gains from executing a set of tests then guides the tester in designing and executing the next set of tests.

- Exploratory testing is vital whenever choosing the next test case to be run cannot be determined in advance but should be chosen based on previous tests and their results.

References

Bach, James. "Exploratory Testing and the Planning Myth."
http://www.stickyminds.com/r.asp?F=DART_2359,
19 March 2001.

Bach, James. "Exploratory Testing Explained." v.1.3 16 April 2003.
http://www.satisfice.com/articles/et-article.pdf

Kaner, Cem, Jack Falk, and Hung Q. Nguyen (1999). *Testing Computer Software*. John Wiley & Sons.

Kaner, Cem, James Bach, and Bret Pettichord (2002). *Lessons Learned in Software Testing: A Context-Driven Approach*. John Wiley & Sons.

Weinberg, Gerald M. (1975). *An Introduction to General Systems Thinking*. John Wiley & Sons.

Chapter 14 –
Test Planning

John Stevenson lives in Vancouver with his wife Cindy and their two kids Shawn and Cassie, who are the second cousins of Mary Shaw, who is married to Richard Shaw, whose grandmother was Stewart Werthington's housekeeper, whose kids Damien and Charlie went to the Mansfield Christian School for Boys with Danny Robinson, whose sister Berta Robinson ran off with Chris Tanner, who rides a motorcycle and greases his hair and their kid Christa used to go out with my pal Tom Slipper, who is the main character of this story, but not the narrator 'cause I am (Tommy couldn't write to save his life).

— Emma Dolan

Introduction

Mort Sahl, the brilliant social commentator of the 1960s, often began his act by dividing the world into the "right wing," the "left wing," and the "social democrats." The previous two chapters have described the right and left wings. Now it's time for the social democrats.

Scripted testing is based on the *sequential* examination of requirements, followed by the design and documentation of test cases, followed by the execution of those test cases. The scripted tester's motto is, "Plan your work, work your plan." Exploratory testing is a very different paradigm. Rather than a sequential approach, exploratory testing emphasizes *concurrent* product learning, test design, and test execution. The tester designs and executes tests while exploring the product.

Technique

Planning has been defined simply as "figuring out what to do next." Most of us would admit that to be effective and efficient, planning is important. But when and how should that planning be done? Scripted testing emphasizes the value of early test planning and design as a method of detecting requirements and design defects before the code is written and the system put into production. Exploratory testing challenges the idea that tests must be designed so very early in the project, when our knowledge is typically at its minimum. In his article, "Exploratory Testing and the Planning Myth," published on StickyMinds.com, James Bach discusses the planning of plays that are run in a football game. He examines when the plays can or should be planned. Let's consider this sport to learn more about planning.

But first, an apology or explanation. In this chapter the term "football" refers to the game of the same name as played in the United States and Canada and exported, with only marginal success, to the rest of the world. "Football" does not refer to that marvelous game played world-wide that North Americans call "soccer."

When are football plays planned? Our first thought might be in the huddle just before the play begins, but the following list shows more possibilities:

- Before the game begins – the first n plays are chosen and executed without regard to their success or failure to evaluate both teams' abilities

- Before each play – in the huddle, based on an overall game plan, field position, teams' strengths and weaknesses, and player skills and experience

- At the line of scrimmage – depending on the defensive lineup

- At the start of a play – play action – run or pass depending on the defense

- During the play – run for your life when all else has failed

We could define the terms "classical planning" and "adaptive planning" to indicate these different approaches. The relationship between classical planning and adaptive planning in football is:

■■■■■■■■■■■■■■■■■■
For More Information

To learn more about the game of football as played in North America see ww2.nfl.com/basics/ history_basics.html

---

■■■■■■■■■■■■■■■■■■
Planned Football Play

■■■■■■■■■■■■■■■■■■
Adaptive Planning

Adaptive planning is not an industry standard term. Other possible terms are:

- Dynamic
- Flexible
- Just-In-Time
- Responsive
- Pliable
- Progressive
- Purposeful planning

Classical Planning	Before the game begins (the first ten plays are scripted)
Adaptive Planning	Before each play (in the huddle)
	At the line of scrimmage (depending on the defensive setup)
	At the start of a play (play action – run or pass)
	During the play (scramble when all else has failed)

■■■■■■■■■■■■■■■■■
Table 14-1

Classical planning vs. Adaptive planning.

___

Let's now leave football and consider software test planning. (While we'd rather stay and watch the game, we've got software to test.)

Classical Test Planning	As requirements, analysis, design, and coding are being done—long before system is built and the testing can begin
Adaptive Test Planning	Choose a strategy (depending on our current knowledge)
	Before each screen / function / flow is to be tested
	At the start of an individual test (choose different strategies)
	During the test (as we observe things we don't expect or understand)

■■■■■■■■■■■■■■■■■
Table 14-2

Classical test planning vs. Exploratory test planning.

___

A reasonable planning heuristic would be:

- We plan as much as we can (based on the knowledge available),
- When we can (based on the time and resources available),
- But not before.

Aside from these new labels, haven't good planners always done this? Is this concept really new?

A remarkable little book simply titled *Planning*, published by the United States Marine Corps in 1997, describes the concepts of adaptive planning in detail.

The Marine Corps defines planning as encompassing two basic functions—"envisioning a desired future and arranging a configuration of potential actions in time and space that will allow us to realize that future." But, to the Marines, planning is not something done early which then becomes cast in concrete. "We should think of planning as a learning process—as mental preparation which improves our understanding of a situation." Plans are not concrete either. "Since planning is an ongoing process, it is better to think of a plan as an interim product based on the information and understanding known at the moment and always subject to revision as new information and understanding emerge."

The authors of *Planning* list these planning pitfalls to avoid:

- Attempting to forecast events too far into the future. By planning we may fool ourselves into thinking we are controlling. There is a difference.

- Trying to plan in too much detail. Helmuth von Moltke, German Army Chief of Staff during World War I said, "No plan survives contact with the enemy." In exactly that same way, no test plan survives contact with the defects in the system under test.

- Institutionalizing planning methods that lead us to inflexible or lockstep thinking in which both planning and plans become rigid. Rather than "Plan your work and work your plan" as our mantra, we should constantly "Plan our work, work our plan, re-evaluate our work, re-evaluate our plan."

- Thinking of a plan as an unalterable solution to a problem. Rather, it should be viewed as an open architecture that allows us to pursue many alternatives. "We will rarely, if ever, conduct an evolution exactly the way it was originally developed."

- Ignoring the need for a feedback mechanism to identify shortcomings in the plan and make necessary adjustments. This is a component of planning which often does not receive adequate emphasis. "Many plans stop short of identifying the signals, conditions, and feedback mechanisms that will indicate successful or dysfunctional execution."

Adaptive planning, as described above, acknowledges and deals with these pitfalls.

The following excerpt from *Planning* summarizes these concepts well:

> "Planning is a continuous process involving the ongoing adjustment of means and ends. We should also view planning as an evolutionary process involving continuous adjustment and improvement. We can think of planning as solution-by-evolution rather than solution-by-engineering. We should generally not view planning as trying to solve a problem in one iteration because most ... problems are too complex to be solved

that way. In many cases, it is more advisable to find a workable solution quickly and improve the solution as time permits. What matters most is not generating the best possible plan but achieving the best possible result. Likewise, we should see each plan as an evolving rather than a static document. Like planning, plans should be dynamic; a static plan is of no value to an adaptive organization in a fluid situation."

Summary

- James Bach asks, "What if it [the plan] comes into existence only moments before the testing?" Why must the plan be created so very early in the project, when our knowledge is typically at its minimum?

- In adaptive planning we plan as much as we can (based on the knowledge available), when we can (based on the time and resources available), but not before.

- Since planning is an ongoing process, it is better to think of a plan as an interim product based on the information and understanding known at the moment and always subject to revision as new information and understanding emerge.

- The use of scripted testing does not preclude the use of exploratory testing. The use of exploratory testing does not preclude the use of scripted testing. As Rex Black wrote, "Smart testers use whatever tool in their toolbox is required. No paradigms here. No worldviews here. No screwdrivers vs. hammers. Let's do whatever makes sense given the problem at hand."

Key Point

The use of scripted testing does not preclude the use of exploratory testing. The use of exploratory testing does not preclude the use of scripted testing. Smart testers use whatever tool in their toolbox is required.

Practice

1. In what areas could you use adaptive planning where you now use classical planning? With what benefit? What would the challenges be? Who would support you in this new process? Who would oppose your efforts? Why?

2. In what movies about the Marine Corps were the process of planning and the value of plans emphasized over action? Can you explain why?

References

Bach, James. "Exploratory Testing and the Planning Myth."
19 March 2001.
http://www.stickyminds.com/r.asp?F=DART_2359

Copeland, Lee. "Exploratory Planning." 3 September 2001.
http://www.stickyminds.com/r.asp?F=DART_2805

"IEEE Standard for Software Test Documentation," IEEE Std
829-1998. The Institute of Electrical and Electronics Engineers,
Inc.
ISBN 0-7381-1443-X

Planning. MCDP 5. United States Marine Corps.
https://www.doctrine.usmc.mil/mcdp/view/mpdpub5.pdf

Section IV –
Supporting Technologies

The Bookends

Two questions, like bookends, frame our software testing:

- Where do we start?
- When do we stop?

Where do we start testing? Of all the places to look for defects, where should we begin? One answer is with a defect taxonomy. A taxonomy is a classification of things into ordered groups or categories that indicate natural, hierarchical relationships. Taxonomies help identify the kinds of defects that often occur in systems, guide your testing by generating ideas, and audit your test plans to determine the coverage you are obtaining with your test cases. In time, they can help you improve your development process.

And stopping. How do we logically decide when we have tested enough and the software is ready for delivery and installation? Boris Beizer has written, "There is no single, valid, rational criterion for stopping." If he is correct, how do we make that decision?

The next two chapters address these important issues.

Chapter 15 –
Defect Taxonomies

'Failure' was simply not a word that would ever cross the lips of Miss Evelyn Duberry, mainly because Evelyn, a haughty socialite with fire-red hair and a coltish gate, could pronounce neither the letters 'f' nor 'r' as a result of an unfortunate kissing gesture made many years earlier toward her beloved childhood parrot, Snippy.

— David Kenyon

Introduction

What is a taxonomy? A taxonomy is a classification of things into ordered groups or categories that indicate natural, hierarchical relationships. The word taxonomy is derived from two Greek roots: "taxis" meaning arrangement and "onoma" meaning name. Taxonomies not only facilitate the orderly storage of information, they facilitate its retrieval and the discovery of new ideas. Taxonomies help you:

- Guide your testing by generating ideas for test design
- Audit your test plans to determine the coverage your test cases are providing
- Understand your defects, their types and severities
- Understand the process you currently use to produce those defects (Always remember, your current process is finely tuned to create the defects you're creating)
- Improve your development process
- Improve your testing process
- Train new testers regarding important areas that deserve testing
- Explain to management the complexities of software testing

In his book *Testing Object-Oriented Systems*, Robert Binder describes a "fault model" as a list of typical defects that occur in systems. Another phrase to describe such a list is a defect taxonomy. Binder then describes two approaches to testing. The first uses a "non-specific fault model." In other words, no defect taxonomy is used. Using this approach, the requirements and specifications guide the creation of all of our test cases. The second approach uses a "specific fault model." In this approach, a taxonomy of defects guides the creation of test cases. In other words, we create test cases to discover faults like the ones we

■■■■■■■■■■■■■■■■■■
Key Point

A taxonomy is a classification of things into ordered groups or categories that indicate natural, hierarchical relationships.

have experienced before. We will consider two levels of taxonomies—project level and software defect level. Of most importance in test design are the software defect taxonomies. But it would be foolish to begin test design before evaluating the risks associated with both the product and its development process.

Note that none of the taxonomies presented below are complete. Each could be expanded. Each is subjective based on the experience of those who created the taxonomies.

Project Level Taxonomies

SEI Risk Identification Taxonomy

The Software Engineering Institute has published a "Taxonomy-Based Risk Identification" that can be used to identify, classify, and evaluate different risk factors found in the development of software systems.

Class	Element	Attribute
Product Engineering	Requirements	Stability
		Completeness
		Clarity
		Validity
		Feasibility
		Precedent
		Scale
	Design	Functionality
		Difficulty
		Interfaces
		Performance
		Testability
	Code and Unit Test	Feasibility
		Testing
		Coding/Implementation
	Integration and Test	Environment
		Product
		System
	Engineering Specialties	Maintainability

■■■■■■■■■■■■■■■■■

Table 15-1

The SEI Taxonomy-Based Risk Identification taxonomy.

		Reliability
		Safety
		Security
		Human Factors
		Specifications
Development Environment	Development Process	Formality
		Suitability
		Process Control
		Familiarity
		Product Control
	Development System	Capacity
		Suitability
		Usability
		Familiarity
		Reliability
		System Support
		Deliverability
	Management Process	Planning
		Project Organization
		Management Experience
		Program Interfaces
	Management Methods	Monitoring
		Personnel Management
		Quality Assurance
		Configuration Management
	Work Environment	Quality Attitude
		Cooperation
		Communication
		Morale
Program Constraints	Resources	Schedule
		Staff
		Budget
		Facilities
	Contract	Types of Contract
		Restrictions
		Dependencies
	Program Interfaces	Customer
		Associate Contractors
		Subcontractors
		Prime Contractor
		Corporate Management
		Vendors
		Politics

If, as a tester, you had concerns with some of these elements and attributes, you would want to stress certain types of testing. For example:

If you are concerned about:	You might want to emphasize:
The stability of the requirements	Formal traceability
Incomplete requirements	Exploratory testing
Imprecisely written requirements	Decision tables and/or state-transition diagrams
Difficulty in realizing the design	Control flow testing
System performance	Performance testing
Lack of unit testing	Additional testing resources
Usability problems	Usability testing

ISO 9126 Quality Characteristics Taxonomy

The ISO 9126 Standard "Software Product Evaluation—Quality Characteristics and Guidelines" focuses on measuring the quality of software systems. This international standard defines software product quality in terms of six major characteristics and twenty-one subcharacteristics and defines a process to evaluate each of these. This taxonomy of quality attributes is:

Quality Characteristic	Subcharacteristic
Functionality (Are the required functions available in the software?)	Suitability
	Accuracy
	Interoperability
	Security
Reliability (How reliable is the software?)	Maturity
	Fault tolerance
	Recoverability
Usability (Is the software easy to use?)	Understandability
	Learnability
	Operability
	Attractiveness
Efficiency (How efficient is the software?)	Time behavior
	Resource behavior
Maintainability (How easy is it to modify the software?)	Analyzability
	Changeability
	Stability
	Testability

■■■■■■■■■■■■■■■■■

Table 15-2

The ISO 9126 Quality Characteristics taxonomy.

Portability (How easy is it to transfer the software to another operating environment?)	Adaptability
	Installability
	Coexistence
	Replaceability

Each of these characteristics and subcharacteristics suggest areas of risk and thus areas for which tests might be created. An evaluation of the importance of these characteristics should be undertaken first so that the appropriate level of testing is performed. A similar "if you are concerned about / you might want to emphasize" process could be used based on the ISO 9126 taxonomy.

These project level taxonomies can be used to guide our testing at a strategic level. For help in software test design we use software defect taxonomies.

Software Defect Taxonomies

In software test design we are primarily concerned with taxonomies of defects, ordered lists of common defects we expect to encounter in our testing.

Beizer's Taxonomy

One of the first defect taxonomies was defined by Boris Beizer in *Software Testing Techniques*. It defines a four-level classification of software defects. The top two levels are shown here.

1xxx	Requirements
11xx	Requirements incorrect
12xx	Requirements logic
13xx	Requirements, completeness

■■■■■■■■■■■■■■■■■

Table 15-3

A portion of Beizer's Bug Taxonomy.

14xx	Verifiability
15xx	Presentation, documentation
16xx	Requirements changes
2xxx	**Features And Functionality**
21xx	Feature/function correctness
22xx	Feature completeness
23xx	Functional case completeness
24xx	Domain bugs
25xx	User messages and diagnostics
26xx	Exception conditions mishandled
3xxx	**Structural Bugs**
31xx	Control flow and sequencing
32xx	Processing
4xxx	**Data**
41xx	Data definition and structure
42xx	Data access and handling
5xxx	**Implementation And Coding**
51xx	Coding and typographical
52xx	Style and standards violations
53xx	Documentation
6xxx	**Integration**
61xx	Internal interfaces
62XX	External interfaces, timing, throughput
7XXX	**System And Software Architecture**
71XX	O/S call and use
72XX	Software architecture
73XX	Recovery and accountability
74XX	Performance
75XX	Incorrect diagnostics, exceptions
76XX	Partitions, overlays
77XX	Sysgen, environment
8XXX	**Test Definition And Execution**
81XX	Test design bugs
82XX	Test execution bugs
83XX	Test documentation
84XX	Test case completeness

Even considering only the top two levels, it is quite extensive. All four levels of the taxonomy constitute a fine-grained framework with which to categorize defects.

At the outset, a defect taxonomy acts as a checklist, reminding the tester so that no defect types are forgotten. Later, the taxonomy can be used as a framework to record defect data. Subsequent analysis of this data can help an organization understand the types of defects it creates, how many (in terms of raw numbers and percentages), and how and why these defects occur. Then, when faced with too many things to test and not enough time, you will have data that enables you to make risk-based, rather than random, test design decisions. In addition to taxonomies that suggest the types of defects that may occur, always evaluate the impact on the customer and ultimately on your organization if they do occur. Defects that have low impact may not be worth tracking down and repairing.

Kaner, Falk, and Nguyen's Taxonomy

The book *Testing Computer Software* contains a detailed taxonomy consisting of over 400 types of defects. Only a few excerpts from this taxonomy are listed here.

User Interface Errors	Functionality
	Communication
	Command structure
	Missing commands
	Performance
	Output
Error Handling	Error prevention
	Error detection
	Error recovery
Boundary-Related Errors	Numeric boundaries
	Boundaries in space, time
	Boundaries in loops
Calculation Errors	Outdated constants
	Calculation errors
	Wrong operation order
	Overflow and underflow
Initial And Later States	Failure to set a data item to 0
	Failure to initialize a loop control variable
	Failure to clear a string
	Failure to reinitialize
Control Flow Errors	Program runs amok
	Program stops
	Loops
	IF, THEN, ELSE or maybe not
Errors In Handling Or Interpreting Data	Data type errors
	Parameter list variables out of order or missing
	Outdated copies of data
	Wrong value from a table
	Wrong mask in bit field

Table 15-4

A portion of the defect taxonomy from *Testing Computer Software*.

Race Conditions	Assuming one event always finishes before another
	Assuming that input will not occur in a specific interval
	Task starts before its prerequisites are met
Load Conditions	Required resource not available
	Doesn't return unused memory
Hardware	Device unavailable
	Unexpected end of file
Source And Version Control	Old bugs mysteriously reappear
	Source doesn't match binary
Documentation	None
Testing Errors	Failure to notice a problem
	Failure to execute a planned test
	Failure to use the most promising test cases
	Failure to file a defect report

Binder's Object-Oriented Taxonomy

Robert Binder notes that many defects in the object-oriented (OO) paradigm are problems using encapsulation, inheritance, polymorphism, message sequencing, and state-transitions. This is to be expected for two reasons. First, these are cornerstone concepts in OO. They form the basis of the paradigm and thus will be used extensively. Second, these basic concepts are very different from the procedural paradigm. Designers and programmers new to OO would be expected to find them foreign ideas. A small portion of Binder's OO taxonomy is given here to give you a sense of its contents:

Method Scope		Fault
Requirements		Requirement omission
Design	Abstraction	Low Cohesion
	Refinement	Feature override missing
		Feature delete missing
	Encapsulation	Naked access
		Overuse of friend
	Responsibilities	Incorrect algorithm
		Invariant violation
	Exceptions	Exception not caught

■■■■■■■■■■■■■■■■■

Table 15-5

A portion of Binder's Method Scope Fault Taxonomy.

Class Scope		Fault
Design	Abstraction	Association missing or incorrect
		Inheritance loops
	Refinement	Wrong feature inherited
		Incorrect multiple inheritance
	Encapsulation	Public interface not via class methods
		Implicit class-to-class communication
	Modularity	Object not used
		Excessively large number of methods
	Implementation	Incorrect constructor

Table 15-6

A portion of Binder's Class Scope Fault Taxonomy.

Note how this taxonomy could be used to guide both inspections and test case design. Binder also references specific defect taxonomies for C++, Java, and Smalltalk.

Whittaker's "How to Break Software" Taxonomy

James Whittaker's book *How to Break Software* is a tester's delight. Proponents of exploratory testing exhort us to "explore." Whittaker tells us specifically "where to explore." Not only does he identify areas in which faults tend to occur, he defines specific testing attacks to locate these faults. Only a small portion of his taxonomy is presented:

Fault Type	Attack
Inputs and outputs	Force all error messages to occur
	Force the establishing of default values
	Overflow input buffers
Data and computation	Force the data structure to store too few or too many values
	Force computation results to be too large or too small
File system interface	Fill the file system to its capacity
	Damage the media
Software interfaces	Cause all error handling code to execute
	Cause all exceptions to fire

Table 15-7

A portion of Whittaker's Fault Taxonomy.

Vijayaraghavan's eCommerce Taxonomy

Beizer's, Kaner's, and Whittaker's taxonomies catalog defects that can occur in any system. Binder's focuses on common defects in object-oriented systems. Giri Vijayaraghavan has chosen a much narrower focus—the eCommerce shopping cart. Using this familiar metaphor, an eCommerce Web site keeps track of the state of a user while shopping. Vijayaraghavan has investigated the many ways shopping carts can fail. He writes, "We developed the list of shopping cart failures to study the use of the outline as a test idea generator." This is one of the prime uses of any defect taxonomy. His taxonomy lists over sixty high-level defect categories, some of which are listed here:

- Performance
- Reliability
- Software upgrades
- User interface usability
- Maintainability
- Conformance
- Stability
- Operability
- Fault tolerance
- Accuracy
- Internationalization
- Recoverability
- Capacity planning
- Third-party software failure
- Memory leaks
- Browser problems
- System security
- Client privacy

After generating the list he concludes, "We think the list is a sufficiently broad and well-researched collection that it can be used as a starting point for testing other applications." His assertion is certainly correct.

A Final Observation

Note that each of these taxonomies is a list of possible defects without any guidance regarding the probability that these will occur in your systems and without any suggestion of the loss your organization would incur if these defects did occur. Taxonomies are useful starting points for our testing but they are certainly not a complete answer to the question of where to start testing.

Your Taxonomy

Now that we have examined a number of different defect taxonomies, the question arises—which is the correct one for you? The taxonomy that is most useful is **your** taxonomy, the one you create from your experience within your organization. Often the place to start is with an existing taxonomy. Then modify it to more accurately reflect your particular situation in terms of defects, their frequency of occurrence, and the loss you would incur if these defects were not detected and repaired.

■■■■■■■■■■■■■■■■■
Key Point

The taxonomy that is most useful is **your** taxonomy, the one you create.

Just as in other disciplines like biology, psychology, and medicine, there is no one, single, right way to categorize, there is no one right software defect taxonomy. Categories may be fuzzy and overlap. Defects may not correspond to just one category. Our list may not be complete, correct, or consistent. That matters very little. What matters is that we are collecting, analyzing, and categorizing our past experience and feeding it forward to improve our ability to detect defects. Taxonomies are merely models and, as George Box, the famous statistician, reminds us, "All models are wrong; some models are useful."

To create your own taxonomy, first start with a list of key concepts. Don't worry if your list becomes long. That may be just fine. Make sure the items in your taxonomy are short, descriptive phrases. Keep your users (that's you and other testers in your organization) in mind. Use terms that are common for them. Later, look for natural hierarchical relationships between items in the taxonomy. Combine these into a major category with subcategories underneath. Try not to duplicate or overlap categories and subcategories. Continue to add new categories as they are discovered. Revise the categories and subcategories when new items don't seem to fit well. Share your taxonomy with others and solicit their feedback. You are on your way to a taxonomy that will contribute to your testing success.

Summary

- Taxonomies help you:
    - Guide your testing by generating ideas for test case design
    - Audit your test plans to determine the coverage your test cases are providing
    - Understand your defects, their types and severities
    - Understand the process you currently use to produce those defects (Always remember, your current process is finely tuned to create the defects you're creating)
    - Improve your development process
    - Improve your testing process
    - Train new testers regarding important areas that deserve testing
    - Explain to management the complexities of software testing

- Testing can be done without the use of taxonomies (non-specific fault model) or with a taxonomy (specific fault model) to guide the design of test cases.

- Taxonomies can be created at a number of levels: generic software system, development paradigm, type of application, and user interface metaphor.

References

Beizer, Boris (1990). *Software Testing Techniques* (Second Edition). Van Nostrand Reinhold.

Binder, Robert V. (2000). *Testing Object-Oriented Systems: Models, Patterns, and Tools.* Addison-Wesley.

Carr, Marvin J., et al. (1993) "Taxonomy-Based Risk Identification." Technical Report CMU/SEI-93-TR-6, ESC-TR-93-183, June 1993. http://www.sei.cmu.edu/pub/documents/93.reports/pdf/tr06.93.pdf

ISO (1991). *ISO/IEC Standard 9126-1. Software Engineering - Product Quality – Part 1: Quality Model,* ISO Copyright Office, Geneva, June 2001.

Kaner, Cem, Jack Falk and Hung Quoc Nguyen (1999). *Testing Computer Software* (Second Edition). John Wiley & Sons.

Whittaker, James A. (2003). *How to Break Software: A Practical Guide to Testing.* Addison Wesley.

Vijayaraghavan, Giri and Cem Kaner. "Bugs in your shopping cart: A Taxonomy." http://www.testingeducation.org/articles/BISC_Final.pdf

Chapter 16 –
When to Stop Testing

The ballerina stood on point, her toes curled like shrimp, not deep-fried shrimp because, as brittle as they are, they would have cracked under the pressure, but tender ebi-kind-of-shrimp, pink and luscious as a Tokyo sunset, wondering if her lover was in the Ginza, wooing the geisha with eyes reminiscent of roe, which she liked better than ebi anyway.

— Brian Tacang

The Banana Principle

In his classic book *An Introduction to General Systems Thinking*, Gerald Weinberg introduces us to the "Banana Principle." A little boy comes home from school and his mother asks, "What did you learn in school today?" The boy responds, "Today we learned how to spell 'banana' but we didn't learn when to stop." In this book we have learned how to design effective and efficient test cases, but how do we know when to stop? How do we know we have done enough testing?

When to Stop

In *The Complete Guide to Software Testing*, Bill Hetzel wrote regarding system testing, "Testing ends when we have measured system capabilities and corrected enough of the problems to have confidence that we are ready to run the acceptance test." The phrases "corrected enough" and "have confidence," while certainly correct, are vague.

Regarding stopping, Boris Beizer has written, "There is no single, valid, rational criterion for stopping. Furthermore, given any set of applicable criteria, how exactly each is weighted depends very much upon the product, the environment, the culture and the attitude to risk." Again, not much help in knowing when to stop testing.

Even though Beizer says there is no single criterion for stopping, many organizations have chosen one anyway. The five basic criteria often used to decide when to stop testing are:

- You have met previously defined coverage goals

- The defect discovery rate has dropped below a previously defined threshold
- The marginal cost of finding the "next" defect exceeds the expected loss from that defect
- The project team reaches consensus that it is appropriate to release the product
- The boss says, "Ship it!"

Coverage Goals

Coverage is a measure of how much has been tested compared with how much is available to test. Coverage can be defined at the code level with metrics such as statement coverage, branch coverage, and path coverage. At the integration level, coverage can be defined in terms of APIs tested or API/parameter combinations tested. At the system level, coverage can be defined in terms of functions tested, use cases (or user stories) tested, or use case scenarios (main path plus all the exception paths) tested. Once enough test cases have been executed to meet the previously defined coverage goals, we are, by definition, finished testing. For example, we could define a project's stopping criteria as:

- 100% statement coverage
- 90% use case scenario coverage

When this number of tests pass, we are finished testing. (Of course, there are many other combinations of factors that could be used as stopping criteria.) Not all testers approve of this approach. Glenford Myers believes that this method is highly counterproductive. He believes that because human beings are very goal oriented, this criterion could subconsciously encourage testers to write test cases that have a low probability of detecting defects but do meet the coverage criteria. He believes that more specific criteria such as a set of tests that cover all boundary values, state-transition events, decision table rules, etc. are superior.

Defect Discovery Rate

Another approach is to use the defect discovery rate as the criteria for stopping. Each week (or other short period of time) we count the number of defects discovered. Typically, the number of defects found each week resembles the curve in Figure 16-1. Once the discovery rate is less than a certain previously selected threshold, we are finished testing. For example, if we had set the threshold at three defects/week, we would stop testing after week 18.

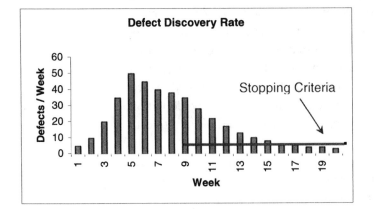

■■■■■■■■■■■■■■■■■■

Figure 16-1

Defect Discovery
Rate

While this approach appeals to our intuition, we should consider what other situations would produce a curve like this—creation of additional, but less effective test cases; testers on vacation; "killer" defects that still exist in the software but that hide very well. This is one reason why Beizer suggests not depending on only one stopping criterion.

Marginal Cost

In manufacturing, we define "marginal cost" as the cost associated with one additional unit of production. If we're making 1,000 donuts, what is the additional cost of making one more? Not very much. In manufacturing, the marginal cost typically decreases as the number of units made increases. In software testing, however, just the opposite occurs. Finding the first few defects is relatively simple and inexpensive. Finding each additional defect becomes more and more time consuming and costly because these defects are very adept at hiding from our test cases. Thus the cost of finding the "next" defect increases. At some point the cost of finding that defect exceeds the loss our organization would incur if we shipped the product with that defect. Clearly, it is (past) time to stop testing.

Not every system should use this criterion. Systems that require high reliability such as weapons systems, medical devices, industrial controls, and other safety-critical systems may require additional testing because of their risk and subsequent loss should a failure occur.

Team Consensus

Based on various factors including technical, financial, political, and just "gut feelings," the project team (managers, developers, testers, marketing, sales, quality assurance, etc.) decide that the benefits of delivering the software now outweigh the potential liabilities and reach consensus that the product should be released.

Ship It!

For many of us, this will be the only strategy we will ever personally experience. It's often very disheartening for testers, especially after many arduous hours of testing, and with a sure knowledge that many defects are still hiding in the software, to be told "Ship it!" What testers must remember is that there may be very reasonable and logical reasons for shipping the product before we, as testers, think it is ready. In today's fast-paced market economy, often the "first to market" wins a substantial market share. Even if the product is less than perfect, it may still satisfy the needs of many users and bring significant profits to our organization; profits that might be lost if we delayed shipment.

Some of the criteria that should be considered in making this decision are the complexity of the product itself, the complexity of the technologies used to implement it and our skills and experience in using those technologies, the organization's culture and the importance of risk aversion in our organization, and the environment within which the system will operate including the financial and legal exposure we have if the system fails.

As a tester, you may be frustrated by the "Ship It" decision. Remember, our role as testers is to inform management of the risks of shipping the product. The role of your organization's marketing and sales groups should be to inform management of the benefits of shipping the product. With this information, both positive and negative, project managers can make informed, rational decisions.

Some Concluding Advice

Lesson 185 in *Lessons Learned in Software Testing* states:

"Because testing is an information gathering process, you can stop when you've gathered enough information. You could stop after you've found every bug, but it would take infinite testing to know that you've found every bug, so that won't work. Instead, you should stop when you reasonably believe that the probability is low that the product still has important undiscovered problems.

"Several factors are involved in deciding that testing is good enough (low enough chance of undiscovered significant bugs):

- You are aware of the kinds of problems that would be important to find, if they existed.
- You are aware of how different parts of the product could exhibit important problems.
- You have examined the product to a degree and in a manner commensurate with these risks.
- Your test strategy was reasonably diversified to guard against tunnel vision.
- You used every resource available for testing.
- You met every testing process standard that your clients would expect you to meet.
- You expressed your test strategy, test results, and quality assessments as clearly as you could."

Summary

- Regarding stopping, Boris Beizer has written, "There is no single, valid, rational criterion for stopping. Furthermore, given any set of applicable criteria, how exactly each is weighted depends very much upon the product, the environment, the culture and the attitude to risk."

- The five basic criteria often used to decide when to stop testing are:

  - You have met previously defined coverage goals
  - The defect discovery rate has dropped below a previously defined threshold
  - The marginal cost of finding the "next" defect exceeds the expected loss from that defect
  - The project team reaches consensus that it is appropriate to release the product
  - The boss says, "Ship it!"

References

Hetzel, Bill (1998). *The Complete Guide to Software Testing* (Second Edition). John Wiley & Sons.

Kaner, Cem, James Bach, and Bret Pettichord (2002). *Lessons Learned in Software Testing: A Context-Driven Approach.* John Wiley & Sons.

Myers, Glenford (1979). *The Art of Software Testing.* John Wiley & Sons.

Weinberg, Gerald M. (1975). *An Introduction to General Systems Thinking*. John Wiley & Sons.

Section V –
Some Final Thoughts

Your Testing Toolbox

My oldest son Shawn is a glazier—he installs glass, mirrors, shower doors, etc. He is an artist in glass. As a father, I decided it would be good to know what my son does for a living, so I rode with him in his truck for a few hours watching him work.

At the first job site he pulled out a clipboard with a work order that told him what was needed. He hopped out and walked around to the back of the truck. There, he grabbed his tool bucket (an old five-gallon paint bucket) and rooted around through it. He pulled out some tools, walked up to the house, did his magic, came back to the truck, put the tools in the bucket, and away we went. At the second job site he repeated the process. Once again, he pulled out the clipboard, hopped out, walked around to the back of the truck, grabbed his tool bucket, and rooted around through it. He pulled out some tools, but different tools this time, walked up to the house, did his magic, came back to the truck, put the tools in the bucket, and away we went. As we went from job to job it occurred to me that all good craftspeople, including software testers, need a bucket of tools. In addition, good craftspeople know which tool to use in which situation. My intent in writing this book was to help put more tools in your personal testing tool bucket and to help you know which tool to use in which situation. Remember, not every tool needs to be used every time.

Now, it's up to you. The next level of skill comes with practice. Famous educator Benjamin Bloom created a taxonomy for categorizing levels of competency in school settings. The first three levels are:

- Knowledge
- Comprehension
- Application

This book has focused on knowledge and comprehension. The "application" is up to you.

Best wishes in your testing ...

References

Bloom, Benjamin S. (1969). *Taxonomy of Educational Objectives: The Classification of Educational Goals*. Longman Group.

Appendix A –
Brown & Donaldson
Case Study

Introduction

B rown & Donaldson (B&D) is a **<u>fictitious</u>** online brokerage firm that you can use to practice the test design techniques presented in this book. B&D was originally created for Software Quality Engineering's Web/eBusiness Testing course (see http://www.sqe.com). The actual B&D Web site is found at http://bdonline.sqe.com. Any resemblance to any actual online brokerage Web site is purely coincidental.

Login

The Login page is the gateway into the B&D site. It requires a legitimate username and password.

Market News

The Market News page is the main page of the B&D site. It contains navigation buttons on the left side of the page, stock performance charts at the top, and news stories of interest to B&D's investors.

Trade

The Trade page allows a B&D client to buy and sell stocks. It contains a buy/sell button, a text box for the stock ticker symbol, a text box for the number of shares to be bought or sold (quantity), and boxes indicating the type of trade.

Symbol Lookup

The Symbol Lookup page is reached from the Trade page. It is used when the B&D client is unsure of the stock ticker symbol and must look it up. It contains one field where the first few characters of the organization's name are entered.

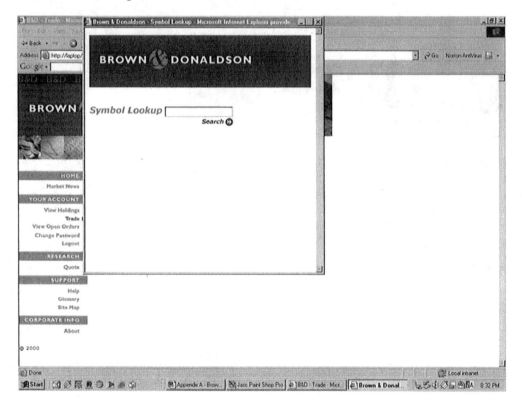

Lookup Results

The Lookup Results page is the result of the previous Symbol
Lookup page. It displays the stock symbols that matched the
previous search.

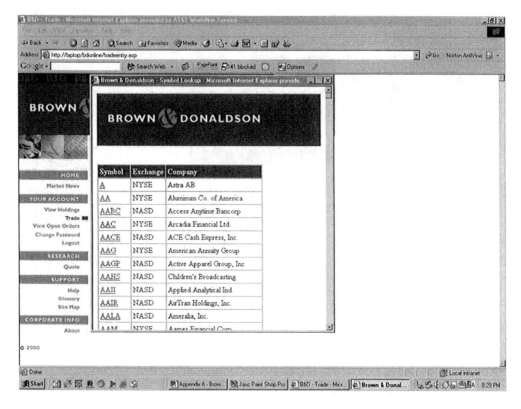

Holdings

Perhaps the most important page on the B&D site, the Holdings page displays the stocks currently owned by this client.

Glossary

The Glossary page can be used to look up terms that unfamiliar to the B&D client.

Appendix B –
Stateless University Registration System Case Study

System Documentation

Stateless University Registration System (SURS)
User Interface Specification
May 1, 2002
Version 2.3

Prepared By:

Otis Kribblekoblis
Super Duper Software Company (SDSC)
422 South 5th Avenue
Anytown, USA

Introduction

The purpose of this document is to describe the planned user interface for the Stateless University Registration System. It will be revised to reflect that "as-built" software after system testing has begun. It is a customized version of the registration system delivered to Universal Online University (UOU) last year. Stateless U has requested some major modifications to the UOU version, so that it is essentially a rewrite of the software. Some of the modules for database creation and backup have been reused, but that is not apparent from the user interface, which is all new.

This manual has the user interface screens defined in the order in which they are customarily used. It starts with the login screen. Then it provides the data base set-up fields: the addition / change / deletion of students, the addition / change / deletion of courses, and the addition / change / deletion of class sections. The final data entry screen provides the selection of specific course sections for each student. There is also an administrative function that is accessible to only the supervisor. It provides access to the administrative functions of backup and restore of the databases. Each screen is defined in a separate section providing the following information:

- Functionality supported
- Formatting requirements for each data entry field
- A sample screen layout (the final implemented software may differ)

The figure below summarizes the screens and their navigation options.

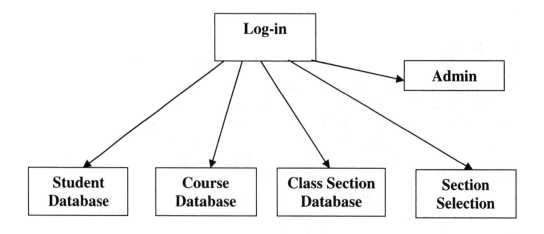

2.1   Log-in and Select Function Screen

2.1.1   Functions

Each user is required to enter a **User ID** and a **Password**. The identification of the status of the user (supervisor: yes or no) is mandatory at the time of log-in. Only **Yes** or **No** may be selected by clicking on the appropriate box (not both). After a successful log-in has been completed, then the next function to be executed can be selected. Only a supervisor may access the Administrative screen. The **Exit** button is active at all times.

2.1.2   Data Entry Formats

The formats for the fields on this screen are:

User ID: eight characters at least two of which are not alphabetic (can be numeric or special characters).

Password: eight characters at least two of which are not alphabetic (can be numeric or special characters).

2.1.3 Screen Format

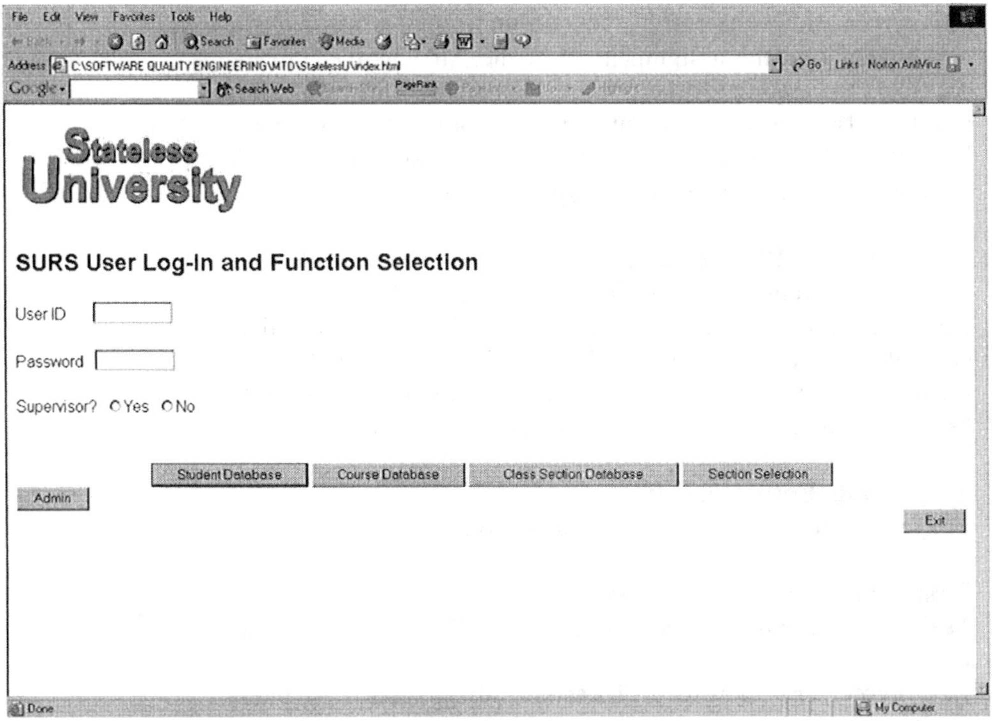

3.1 Student Database Maintenance Screen

3.1.1   Functions

This screen allows the entry of the identifying information for a new student and the assignment of his/her student ID number. All fields are required to be filled in before the **Enter** button is selected. The fields may be entered in any order. The backspace key will work at any time in any field, but the **Reset** button will clear all of the fields when it is pressed.

If the **Student ID** is entered first, then the **Delete** (allows a student to be removed from the database) and **Modify** (allows the modification of the student's contact information—the data currently in the database will be displayed) buttons become active. The **Enter** button will cause the **Delete** or the **Modify** to be executed and the fields on the screen to be cleared.

3.1.2   Data Entry Formats

The formats for the fields (all mandatory) on this screen are:

First name: one to ten characters
Middle name: one to ten characters or NMN for no middle name
Last name: one to fifteen characters (alpha, period, hyphen, apostrophe, space, numbers)
Street address: four to twenty alphanumeric characters
City: three to ten alpha characters
State: two alpha characters
Zip: the standard five numerics hyphen four numerics
Phone: telephone number in the following format 703.555.1212

Student ID: two characters representing the home campus and a six-digit number which is unique for each student. The home campus designations are:

- AN for Annandale
- LO for Loudoun
- MA for Manassas

- WO for Woodbridge
- AR for Arlington

The six-digit number is generated by the system when the **Enter** button is selected. It remains displayed until the **Reset** button is depressed. At that time, all fields are cleared for the next set of entries.

3.1.3   Screen Layout

3.2 Course Database Maintenance Screen

3.2.1 Functions

This screen allows the entry of the identifying information for a new course and the assignment of the course ID number. All fields are required to be filled in before the **Enter** button is pressed. The fields may be entered in any order. The backspace key will work at any time in any field, but the **Reset** button will clear all of the fields when it is entered. The **Back** button causes a return to the previous screen. The **Exit** button causes an exit from this application.

If the **Course ID** is entered first, then the **Delete** (allows a course to be removed from the database) and **Modify** (allows the modification of an existing course's information—the data currently in the database will be displayed) buttons become active. The **Enter** button will cause the **Delete** or the **Modify** to be executed and the fields on the screen to be cleared.

3.2.2 Data Entry Formats

The formats for the fields (all are mandatory) on this screen are:

Course ID: three alpha characters representing the department followed by a six-digit integer which is the unique course identification number. The possible departments are:

- PHY – Physics
- EGR – Engineering
- ENG – English
- LAN – Foreign languages
- CHM – Chemistry
- MAT – Mathematics
- PED – Physical education
- SOC – Sociology
- LIB – Library science
- HEC – Home economics

Course name: a free format alphanumeric field of up to forty characters

Course description: a free format alphanumeric field of up to 250 characters

3.2.3   Screen Layout

3.3 Class Section Database Maintenance Screen

3.3.1 Functions

This screen allows the entry of the identifying information for a new course section. All fields are required to be filled in before the **Enter** button is pressed. The fields may be entered in any order. The backspace key will work at any time in any field, but the **Reset** button will clear all of the fields when it is entered. The **Back** button causes a return to the previous screen. The **Exit** button causes an exit from this application.

The **Course ID** is required to be entered first (all existing sections will be displayed as soon as it is entered), followed by the new **Section #, Dates** and **Time** fields. The **Delete** (allows a section to be removed from the database) and **Modify** (allows the modification of an existing section's information) buttons become active after the **Section #** is entered. If the section is already in the database, the current information will be displayed as soon as the **Section #** field is filled in. The **Enter** button will cause the **Delete** or the **Modify** to be executed and the fields on the screen to be cleared.

3.3.2 Data Entry Formats

The formats for the fields (all mandatory) on this screen are:

Course ID: three alpha characters representing the department followed by a six-digit integer
Section #: a three-digit integer (leading zeros are required) assigned by the user

Dates: the days of the week the class meets (up to three with hyphens in between); the weekday designations are:

- Sun
- Mon
- Tue
- Wed
- Thr

- Fri
- Sat

Time: the starting and ending times of the section (using military time) with a hyphen in between, e.g., 12:00-13:30.

3.3.3 Screen Layout

3.4 Section Selection Entry Screen

3.4.1   Functions
This screen allows the entry of the selection of specific course sections for an individual student. All fields are required to be filled in before the **Enter** button is pressed. The fields may be entered in any order. The backspace key will work at any time in any field, but the **Reset** button will clear all of the fields when it is entered. The **Back** button causes a return to the previous screen. The **Exit** button causes an exit from this application.

The **Student ID** is required to be entered first, followed by the **Course ID** (all available sections will be displayed as soon as it is entered). Sections are selected by clicking on the section to be assigned. The **Enter** button will cause the student to be added to the selected section. Entering a new **Course ID** will cause a new list of available sections to be displayed, allowing another course section to be selected for the same student.

3.4.2   Data Entry Formats
The formats for the fields (all mandatory) on this screen are:

Course ID: three alpha characters representing the department followed by a six-digit integer
Student ID: two characters representing the home campus and a six-digit number that is unique for each student
Available sections: a list of all of the sections that are not full

3.4.3 Screen Layout

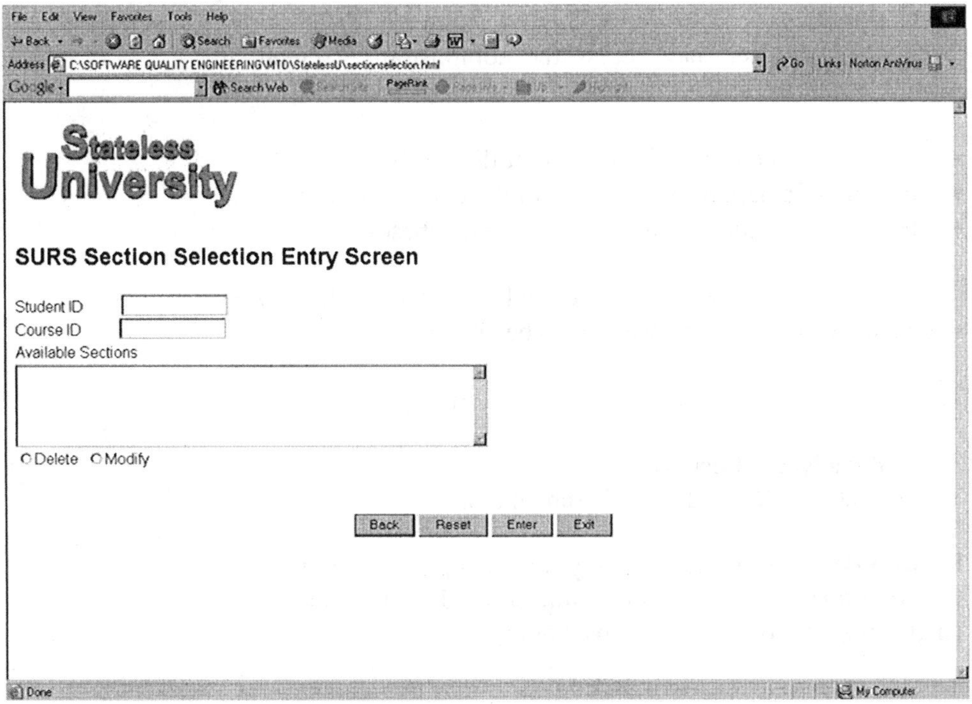

3.5 Administrative Screen

3.5.1 Functions
Only the supervisor may access the administrative screen. It permits one of the following three activities at a time:

- Creation of a backup of any or all of the databases
- Restore of a backup of any or all of the databases
- Printing of a report of any or all of the databases

After the activity (create or restore) and the databases have been selected, the name of the backup is to be entered.

The Back and Exit buttons are active at all times.

3.5.2 Data Entry Formats
The formats for the fields on this screen are:

Backup ID: aannnn (required only for backups, not reports)
Commentary: a free format character field 200 characters in length (required only for backups, not reports)

3.5.3   Screen Layout

Bibliography

Works Cited

Bach, James. "Exploratory Testing and the Planning Myth." 19 March 2001.
http://www.stickyminds.com/r.asp?F=DART_2359

Bach, James. "Exploratory Testing Explained." v.1.3, 16 April 2003.
http://www.satisfice.com/articles/et-article.pdf

Beizer, Boris (1990). *Software Testing Techniques* (Second Edition). Van Nostrand Reinhold. ISBN 0-442-20672-0.

Beizer, Boris (1995). *Black-Box Testing: Techniques for Functional Testing of Software and Systems*. John Wiley & Sons. ISBN 0-471-12094-4.

Binder, Robert V. (2000). *Testing Object-Oriented Systems: Models, Patterns, and Tools*. Addison-Wesley. ISBN 0-201-80938-9.

Brownlie, Robert, et al. "Robust Testing of AT&T PMX/StarMAIL Using OATS," *AT&T Technical Journal*, Vol. 71, No. 3, May/June 1992.

Carr, Marvin J., et al. (1993) *Taxonomy-Based Risk Identification*. Technical Report CMU/SEI-93-TR-6, ESC-TR-93-183, June 1993.
http://www.sei.cmu.edu/pub/documents/93.reports/pdf/tr06.93.pdf

Cockburn, Alistair (2000). *Writing Effective Use Cases*. Addison-Wesley. ISBN 0-201-70225-8.

Cohen, D.M., et al. "The AETG System: An Approach to Testing Based on Combinatorial Design." *IEEE Transactions on Software Engineering*, Vol. 23, No. 7, July 1997.

Copeland, Lee. "Exploratory Planning." 3 September 2001. http://www.stickyminds.com/r.asp?F=DART_2805

Craig, Rick D. and Stefan P. Jaskiel (2002). *Systematic Software Testing*. Artech House Publishers. ISBN 1-58053-508-9.

Fowler, Martin and Kendall Scott (1999). *UML Distilled: A Brief Guide to the Standard Object Modeling Language (2nd Edition)*. Addison-Wesley. ISBN 0-201-65783X.

Gilb, Tom and Dorothy Graham (1993). *Software Inspection*. Addison-Wesley. ISBN 0-201-63181-4.

Harel, David. "Statecharts: a visual formalism for complex systems." *Science of Computer Programming 8*, 1987.

Hetzel, Bill (1998). *The Complete Guide to Software Testing (Second Edition)*. John Wiley & Sons. ISBN 0-471-56567-9.

IEEE Standard for Software Test Documentation: IEEE Standard 829-1998. ISBN 0-7381-1443-X.

IEEE Standard Glossary of Software Engineering Terminology: IEEE Standard 610.12-1990. ISBN 1-55937-067-X.

ISO (1991). *ISO/IEC Standard 9126-1. Software Engineering - Product Quality – Part 1: Quality Model*. ISO Copyright Office, Geneva, June 2001.

Jacobsen, Ivar, et al (1992). *Object-Oriented Systems Engineering: A Use Case Driven Approach*. Addison-Wesley. ISBN 0-201-54435-0.

Kaner, Cem, Jack Falk and Hung Quoc Nguyen (1999). *Testing Computer Software* (Second Edition). John Wiley & Sons. ISBN 0-471-35846-0.

Kaner, Cem, James Bach, and Bret Pettichord (2002). *Lessons Learned in Software Testing: A Context-Driven Approach*. John Wiley & Sons. ISBN 0-471-08112-4.

Kuhn, D. Richard and Michael J. Reilly. "An Investigation of the Applicability of Design of Experiments to Software Testing," 27th NASA/IEEE Software Engineering Workshop, NASA Goddard Space Flight Center, 4-6 December 2002. http://csrc.nist.gov/staff/kuhn/kuhn-reilly-02.pdf

Marick, Brian (1995). *The Craft of Software Testing: Subsystem Testing Including Object-Based and Object-Oriented Testing*. Prentice-Hall. ISBN 0-131-77411-5.

Mandl, Robert. "Orthogonal Latin Squares: An Application of Experiment Design to Compiler Testing," *Communications of the ACM,* Vol. 128, No. 10, October 1985.

Mealy, G.H. "A method for synthesizing sequential circuits." *Bell System Technical Journal*, 34(5): 1955.

Myers, Glenford (1979). *The Art of Software Testing*. John Wiley & Sons. ISBN 0-471-04328-1.

Moore, E.F. "Gedanken-experiments on sequential machines," *Automata Studies* (C. E. Shannon and J. McCarthy, eds.), Princeton, New Jersey: Princeton University Press, 1956.

Phadke, Madhav S. (1989). *Quality Engineering Using Robust Design*. Prentice-Hall. ISBN 0-13-745167-9.

Planning, MCDP 5. United States Marine Corps.
https://www.doctrine.usmc.mil/mcdp/view/mpdpub5.pdf

Pressman, Roger S. (1982). *Software Engineering: A Practitioner's Approach* (Fourth Edition). McGraw-Hill. ISBN 0-07-052182-4.

Rapps, Sandra and Elaine J. Weyuker. "Data Flow Analysis Techniques For Test Data Selection." Sixth International Conference on Software Engineering, Tokyo, Japan, September 13-16, 1982.

Rumbaugh, James, et al. (1991). *Object-Oriented Modeling and Design.* Prentice-Hall. ISBN 0-13-629841-9.

Watson, Arthur H. and Thomas J. McCabe. *Structured Testing: A Testing Methodology Using the Cyclomatic Complexity Metric.* NIST Special Publication 500-235.
http://www.mccabe.com/nist/nist_pub.php

Wallace, Delores R. and D. Richard Kuhn. "Failure Modes in Medical Device Software: An Analysis of 15 Years of Recall Data," *International Journal of Reliability, Quality, and Safety Engineering,* Vol. 8, No. 4, 2001.
http://csrc.nist.gov/staff/kuhn/final-rqse.pdf

Weinberg, Gerald M. (1975). *An Introduction to General Systems Thinking.* John Wiley & Sons.
ISBN 0-471-92563-2.

Whittaker, James A. (2003). *How to Break Software: A Practical Guide to Testing.* Addison Wesley. ISBN 0-201-79619-8.

Other Useful Publications

Beizer, Boris (1984). *Software System Testing and Quality Assurance*. Van Nostrand Reinhold. ISBN 0-442-21306-9.

Black, Rex (1999). *Managing the Testing Process*. Microsoft Press. ISBN 0-7356-0584-X.

British Computer Society. *Standard on Software Component Testing*. BS 7925-2.
http://www.testingstandards.co.uk
http://www.testingstandards.com/BS7925_3_4.zip

Kit, Edward (1995). *Software Testing in the Real World: Improving the Process*. Addison-Wesley. ISBN 0-201-87756-2.

McGregor, John D. and David A. Sykes (2001). *A Practical Guide to Testing Object-Oriented Software*. Addison-Wesley. ISBN 0-201-32564-0.

Meyer, Bertrand (2000). *Object-Oriented Software Construction (2nd Edition)*. Prentice-Hall. ISBN 0-136-29155-4.

Roper, Marc (1994). *Software Testing*. McGraw-Hill. ISBN 0-07-707466-1.

Tamres, Louise (2002). *Introducing Software Testing*. Addison-Wesley. ISBN 0-201-71974-6.

Index

A

B

C

Recent Titles in the Artech House Computing Library

For further information on these and other Artech House titles, including previously considered out-of-print books now available through our In-Print-Forever® (IPF®) program, contact:

Artech House
685 Canton Street
Norwood, MA 02062
Phone: 781-769-9750
Fax: 781-769-6334
e-mail: artech@artechhouse.com

Artech House
46 Gillingham Street
London SW1V 1AH UK
Phone: +44 (0)20 7596-8750
Fax: +44 (0)20 7630-0166
e-mail: artech-uk@artechhouse.com

Find us on the World Wide Web at:
www.artechhouse.com